One Marshal's Badge

RELATED TITLES FROM POTOMAC BOOKS

Spymaster: My Life in the CIA
by Ted Shackley and Richard A. Finney

On-Scene Commander: From Street Agent to Deputy Director of the FBI
by Weldon L. Kennedy

Thinking Like a Terrorist: Insights of a Former FBI Undercover Agent
by Mike German

One Marshal's Badge

A Memoir of Fugitive Hunting, Witness Protection, and the U.S. Marshals Service

LOUIE MCKINNEY
with Pat Russo

Potomac Books, Inc.
Washington, D.C.

Published in the United States by Potomac Books, Inc. All rights reserved. No part of this book may be reproduced in any manner whatsoever without written permission from the publisher, except in the case of brief quotations embodied in critical articles and reviews.

Library of Congress Cataloging-in-Publication Data

McKinney, Louie, 1936–

One marshal's badge : a memoir of fugitive hunting, witness protection, and the U.S. Marshals Service / Louie McKinney, with Pat Russo. — 1st ed.

p. cm.

Includes index.

ISBN 978-1-59797-367-0 (hbk. : alk. paper)

1. McKinney, Louie, 1936– 2. United States. Marshals Service. 3. United States marshals—Biography. 4. Law enforcement—United States—Biography. I. Russo, Pat. II. Title.

HV8144.M37M35 2009

363.28'2092—dc22

[B]

2009019798

Printed in the United States of America on acid-free paper that meets the American National Standards Institute Z39-48 Standard.

Potomac Books, Inc.
22841 Quicksilver Drive
Dulles, Virginia 20166

First Edition

10 9 8 7 6 5 4 3 2 1

An energetic, barefoot boy dashes around the family farm in Walhalla, South Carolina.

He's rushing the cows through an early morning milking, gulping down his breakfast, and heading off to school.

He's sneaking off to places he shouldn't go, fighting with his cousins, and—not surprisingly—getting another whipping from his dad.

At night, he gazes at the long road stretching ahead of him, feeling bewildered and unfulfilled, wondering where his life journey will lead.

Contents

Foreword   ix

Acknowledgments   xi

 1. Introduction   1
 2. Early Years: From the Farm to the High Seas   7
 3. Tales of Two Badges: The D.C. Metropolitan Police
    Department and the U.S. Marshals Service   25
 4. Before Con Air: Transporting Criminals in My Car   41
 5. A Long Bus Ride: Enforcing Integration in the South   49
 6. Preventing Airline Hijackings: The First Sky Marshals   57
 7. Shadow Stalkers: The Creation of the Special Operations
    Group   73
 8. Inventing Identities: The Witness Protection Program   105
 9. Deputy in Paradise: Rising through the Ranks in the
    U.S. Virgin Islands   129
10. Interpol: Helping to Police the World   145
11. Top Cop: Running the Marshals' Fugitive Apprehension
    Operation   157
12. Working Retirement: Leading the Marshals Service   173

Index   191
About the Authors   197

Foreword

During the years that I've been hosting *America's Most Wanted*, I've worked closely with many local, state, and federal law-enforcement agencies. Without a doubt, the U.S. Marshals Service, with its long and successful record for tracking down fugitives, is one of the nation's best.

Through the cases we describe on the show, I've learned that tracking fugitives is typically a long and complicated process. There is always much more to a case than what we can describe in a sixty-minute program. Trails become hard to follow, evidence is spotty and inconsistent, and there often isn't much to go on. Even the best investigators become discouraged after working on a case for months or years, seemingly hunting for a needle in a haystack. Despite the many obstacles, the Marshals Service always manages to pull off the impossible.

In this book, former acting director and Enforcement Operations Division chief Louie McKinney offers a behind-the-scenes look at these veteran fugitive hunters and paints a clear picture of the service's radical transformation. His long tenure with the Marshals also enables him to provide a personal tour of a wealth of investigative and pioneering efforts, including the development of the Witness Protection Program, which has become a valuable tool for many prosecutors.

But his book is much more than one cop's tales of gritty cases. It's an encounter with our country's recent history—from dealing with forced busing and segregation to responding to takeovers and terrorist acts. And it's the inspiring personal story of how one man overcame a life of poverty and hardship.

Louie and I first met during the early years of the show, and I benefited from his help on many of the cases that we profiled. We became fast friends. He has a wealth of experiences, insights, and good stories to share that make for great reading. It's my distinct pleasure to recommend his book to you.

John Walsh
Host, *America's Most Wanted*

Acknowledgments

So many friends and coworkers have encouraged me to write this book over the years that it would take another book just to thank all of you appropriately. Each of you has my sincere thanks and my undying friendship.

A very special thanks to the following individuals, who provided the practical support needed to create this finished product:

Jen Urlock, who gave her "dad" a tape recorder and the instructions that I needed to get started, and who devoted many hours to transcribing my ramblings without accepting a penny for her work.

Andrea Hyllier, who provided so much encouragement, even offering to write and outline this story for me, despite her demanding work-related obligations.

Ed Stubbs, who supported me by reminding me that I needed to get it done before I was too old to remember anything!

Cec Murphey, who connected me with the right person to help me write my memoir. Pat Russo did a marvelous job of listening, organizing, and finding just the right words to communicate my story, but I never would have found him without you!

Introduction

On a quiet Sunday afternoon in November 1981, John Hinckley—the man who shot President Ronald Reagan—hanged himself in his jail cell. The phone call that delivered this information to my suburban Maryland home ended my plans for a relaxing weekend. Because I was in charge of the detail guarding Hinckley, I quickly forgot about watching the rest of the Redskins game.

Shock was my first reaction, followed by a flood of questions about how this could have happened. While speaking with the deputy who called with this news, we made arrangements to quickly get me to the stockade at Fort Meade where Hinckley was held. One persistent thought kept bothering me, however. I wondered whether this unfortunate event would end my otherwise successful career with the U.S. Marshals Service.

After five years as a police officer in Washington, D.C., I'd joined the Marshals Service, where I was steadily moving up the ranks. The son of a sharecropper from the segregated South, I'd already achieved more than I had ever imagined. Now I worried that it might all be going up in smoke.

The noise of an approaching chopper helped me to push this troubling possibility aside and remain focused on my duties. When I stepped aboard the helicopter that landed in the school adjacent to my backyard, I wasn't thinking about my neighbors' reactions to my trip; I focused only on the questions surrounding this incident. As we flew over the rooftops, I watched as the people and the houses got smaller. But those nagging thoughts about my future with the Marshals Service refused to shrink or go away.

When twenty-five-year-old Hinckley shot President Reagan on March 30, 1981, I was assigned to the service's Witness Protection Program, where I was working as an operations officer. While this unit of the Marshals Service is known for its role in providing mob informants with new identities, we're also called upon to provide security during high-profile trials. The administration still wasn't positive whether Hinckley was part of a larger conspiracy, so the attorney general, William French Smith, decided against holding him in a federal prison, where he might be harmed by other inmates or by anyone else who wanted him silenced. Perhaps Smith didn't want history to repeat itself. Lee Harvey Oswald, who was suspected of killing President John F. Kennedy in 1963, had been shot inside a garage at police headquarters while Dallas police officers were preparing to transport him to the county jail.

Guarding prisoners about to stand trial was nothing new to the U.S. Marshals Service. We have been closely attached to the federal courts for our entire history. By ensuring that the courts can operate, we have preserved our constitutional right to trial for more than two hundred years. We have provided protection for federal judges, juries, and attorneys. We have provided the same protection to accused murderers, drug dealers, and terrorists. Protecting John Hinckley was just another part of being a deputy U.S. marshal.

But now that Hinckley had hanged himself, I wondered if perhaps I should start thinking of myself as a "former" deputy U.S. marshal. After all, I had been warned.

Since keeping his location secret would help to safeguard him, we routinely moved Hinckley between facilities, relying on military helicopters to transport him between locations. When he was first arrested, he was kept at the Butner Correctional Facility in Butner, North Carolina. The large medical facilities at Butner made it easy for psychiatric evaluations from doctors hired by the defense and the prosecution. At other times, we kept Hinckley in a cell at the Quantico Marine Corps Base in Quantico, Virginia, as well as at other facilities.

Since it was also important not to let the news media disclose where

Hinckley was, we'd land in a secure area before taking him to a prison. Somehow a reporter learned when we were moving him to the base in Virginia. The next day the *Washington Post* had our pictures on the front page, along with the embarrassing headline, "Hinckley Is Transferred to Brig at Quantico." The rest of the media picked up the story, and we quickly moved Hinckley to Fort Meade, Maryland. We were shocked that we had failed to keep his location a secret.

After that unwanted publicity, the associate director of the Marshals Service—William Hall—told me that he'd gotten a call from the attorney general. Hall was given very clear orders to make sure that nothing happened to Hinckley. Smith told Hall that if anything happened, he'd be looking for a new job. Hall told me that his last official act would be to relieve me of mine.

Apparently, Hinckley jammed his cell door by reaching around the bars and putting the cardboard top from a box of crackers into the lock mechanism. Even though our deputies could put the key into the lock, it refused to budge. We eventually had to call the fire department to open it with bolt cutters.

After he jammed the door, Hinckley cleverly used his jacket to create a noose. When the deputies realized that they couldn't get into the cell to stop him, Roger Mullis, a quick-thinking deputy, ran outside, stuck his hand through the cellblock window, and cut Hinckley down. Before I got there, the deputies had already transported Hinckley to the base hospital. In all of the confusion, no one had told me that he was alive.

When I arrived at the hospital, Hinckley's attorney, Vincent Fuller, was already suggesting that his client was unfit to stand trial, saying that the hanging had likely impaired his memory. If Hinckley had no memory of his actions, a trial would be useless. Rather than argue with Fuller, Robert Chapman, the U.S. attorney who was assisting prosecutor Roger Adelman, made a strategic choice. He decided to see exactly how much Hinckley remembered.

Looking at me, he said, "Louie, you've been with him a lot. Let's see if he remembers you."

I pushed open the door to Hinckley's hospital room and walked in. As soon as he heard me entering the room, he looked up. "Hi, Louie," he said.

"What are you doing here?" That incident wasn't enough to stop his lawyer from questioning Hinckley's mental fitness, however. Weeks of medical and psychiatric evaluations ensued before a trial began.

During the year I spent guarding him, I began to feel sorry for Hinckley. He was so obviously deluded: he had mistaken actress Jodie Foster for the character Iris, the role she played in the 1976 movie *Taxi Driver*, and thought that killing the president would impress her. Before he shot President Reagan, Hinckley saw *Taxi Driver* many times and became obsessed with Foster. He stalked her when she attended Yale University. He even signed up for a class there, sent her letters, called her, and slipped poems under her door. Since she didn't encourage these romantic overtures, he sought another way to get her attention. Because the protagonist in the movie, Travis Bickle, played by Robert De Niro, planned to kill another character who was running for office, Hinckley thought an assassination would impress the object of his affections.

When Foster testified about her interactions with Hinckley during a closed, videotaped session, he was overjoyed to be in the same room with her. When she said that she had no relationship with him, he stood up, shouted a threatening remark at her, and threw a pen in her direction. We quickly removed him from the room and put him in a holding cell in another part of the courthouse. He was visibly upset for quite a while.

When the same videotape was later played in open court for the jury, Hinckley's behavior was no better. From the moment the tape started, he began fidgeting. When he again heard Foster say that she had no relationship with him, he jumped from his chair and ran toward the door. We caught him before he made it very far and put him in the holding cell until he calmed down.

The incident on that Sunday afternoon in November wasn't Hinckley's first suicide attempt, and it wouldn't be his last. He'd taken a number of Tylenol® tablets while at Butner Correctional Facility. When his trial ended in 1982, Hinckley was found not guilty by reason of insanity and held at St. Elizabeths Hospital. In 1983, while he was a patient at St. Elizabeths, he again attempted suicide with an overdose of pills.

When he attempted to hang himself, I'd been with the U.S. Marshals Service for more than ten years. I'd arrested bail jumpers and prison escapees, served as a sky marshal and as part of the elite Special Operations Group, and dealt with a variety of mob informants during the earliest days of the Witness Protection Program. I had no desire to work anywhere else.

Most people are only familiar with a mixture of fact and fiction about the service from TV shows and movies about the Wild West. Mention the U.S. Marshals and they think of Wyatt Earp and the gunfight at the O.K. Corral—even though Wyatt's brother Virgil deputized him only minutes before this famous battle. They might think of the fictional character of Marshal Matt Dillon from the TV series *Gunsmoke* or of the real-life Bat Masterson, a deputy marshal in Kansas, who was famous for his swanky clothes. The modern U.S. Marshals Service has grown far beyond these frontier days; its many impressive accomplishments go far beyond the finest Hollywood scripts or the best-known folklore.

President Reagan described the role of the Marshals Service quite well when he spoke at our national conference in 1985. "Virtually every federal law-enforcement initiative involves the Marshals Service," he said. "If a federal criminal jumps bail, violates parole, or escapes from prison, tracking him down and recapturing him is your responsibility. When an order is issued by a federal court, it's your job to see the order is carried out. You're protecting the courts, judges, attorneys and witnesses and overseeing dozens of tasks essential to the functioning of the justice service. This all adds up to a heavy burden of responsibility."*

The hardworking Marshals Service is not as well known or as large as the Federal Bureau of Investigation (FBI) or the Bureau of Alcohol, Tobacco, and Firearms (ATF). Yet it has broader arrest powers than any law-enforcement agency and makes more arrests than all other federal agencies combined. In 2006 alone, the marshals captured 38,000 federal fugitives. By working in task forces with state and local agencies, we locked up another 46,800.

The U.S. Marshals Service has been relied on whenever the country has needed its unique blend of law-enforcement skills. Marshals enforced

---

*   "Ronald Reagan: Honorary Marshal," *United States Marshals Service: Historical Perspective*, http://www.usmarshals.gov/history/reagan/.

Prohibition during the 1920s, supported the integration of the South during the civil rights era, managed the Witness Protection Program, and provided protection to athletes during the Olympic Games. These accomplishments only begin to describe why I'm so proud of my association with the service.

When John Hinckley attempted suicide, I didn't lose my position with the Marshals. As my career continued, it provided me with the rare privilege of becoming the first career deputy to ever lead the service.

During my career with the Marshals, I was an eyewitness to history. I was involved in forced busing in the South and the American Indian Movement's occupation of Wounded Knee. I relocated mob informants and transported dangerous prisoners. I was shot at, spent days with hired killers, and was trained to fight and kill with my bare hands, if necessary. I traveled to places that I never knew existed, accomplished things that still excite me, and met many interesting and celebrated people.

As the son of a sharecropper from South Carolina, I never dreamed that I'd be running a federal law-enforcement agency. Thanks to the support of my family and friends, I persevered through the tough times and have achieved much more than I ever thought possible.

2
Early Years
From the Farm to the High Seas

Nothing about my early life in Walhalla, South Carolina, offered a single clue about my professional future. The sharpest investigator would not discover a shred of evidence to indicate that this poor country boy would someday enjoy a successful career at the top of a leading law-enforcement agency. Whenever I look back on my childhood, I'm still surprised at the path that my life has taken. In many ways I had the odds stacked against me. I experienced early exposure to family hardship, constant farmwork, and poverty. Because I was an African American, I also had to deal with segregated southern life.

A midwife assisted with my birth on the family farm in Westminster, South Carolina, on April 2, 1936. My dad didn't own the farm; he was what was known as a sharecropper. In return for working the land, half of everything he grew went to the landowner. When I was seven, our family moved to Walhalla, about ten miles north of Westminster, because the soil there was better for farming.

Family photos show my mother—whose name was Christine—as a beautiful woman. The earliest memory—in fact the only memory—that I have of her is from the day that she died. I was in the house with her, sitting on the kitchen floor, doing my best to put wood in the stove to help her get dinner started. I was only a few years old at the time, but I remember clearly that she was planning to serve green beans and potatoes that day. While she was sitting in a chair and breaking up the beans, she began making rather funny noises. When I looked up at her, foam was coming out of her mouth. Frightened, I began crying and hollering, which brought my older sister Elsie into the room. Elsie took one look at mother and ran to fetch our father, who had the mules hitched up and was plowing the fields. My father ran in, quickly picked up my mother, and carried her away to another part of the house. When I awoke the next morning, my mother's bed was outside, which was the custom when someone died in those days. No one ever slept in the bed again; it was taken away by the junk men and burned. Years later I learned that mother had had a stroke. She had also been carrying another child.

There were nine of us growing up on the farm: four boys and five girls. After mother's death, my sisters—Jannie, Doris, Roxie, Elsie, and Carrleine—took charge of the chores. They washed our clothes, sewed sacks into shirts for us to wear, cooked, and cleaned. As the oldest child, Jannie led the effort, despite the polio that had hampered her from birth. Each of my sisters also did their best to provide whatever mothering the younger children needed. They did a remarkable job. My sister Roxie was even referred to as "Mother" by Bobby, the youngest of our clan.

My oldest brother William was appropriately named after my father. William was like a surrogate father for the younger children, and I remember him always working in the fields. Of course, I wanted to be wherever my big brother was, doing whatever he was doing. One day I saw William hitching up the wagon and ran to join him. Seeing that I wanted to come along, he shook his head and ordered me to stay home. Curious about his destination, I ran behind the wagon, trying to stay out of sight in the bushes. When he spotted me and realized that I hadn't listened, he grabbed a short vine and gave me a whipping. Like my father, William was a stern, no-nonsense person.

Despite the size of our family, I never favored one brother or sister over another and I don't recall any childhood rivalries. Throughout our lives, we remained an extremely close-knit group and always looked out for each other. While I may have gotten along fine with my brothers and sisters, that peacefulness didn't extend to my cousins. My father's sisters—Ida and Jessie—regularly brought over huge plates of fried chicken, mashed potatoes, and collard greens on Sundays, and we spent the day together. While the adults sat around the table talking, the children were outside playing hopscotch and baseball and riding horses. Nearly every one of these extended-family gatherings seemed to include me picking a fight with one of my cousins and typically ended with a whipping from my father. I can't recall what prompted my violent tendencies; I only recall that this seemed to be a regular part of my younger days. I was a hotheaded boy; it didn't take much to set me off.

One day a cousin happened to be nearby when my brother William told me to set the brake on the wagon. When my cousin rushed to the brake ahead of me, I instantly began pummeling him. Just as quickly, William grabbed me by the collar and snapped me back in line. "Boy," he told me sternly, "you can't be doing that!" It didn't matter what William said or how many times my father took me to the woodshed; I was always ready for a fight. Thankfully, I would eventually develop the discipline that kept me from behaving this way later in life.

The farmwork was hard and it was constant. We tended crops including peanuts, potatoes, okra, corn, squash, sugarcane, and green beans. There were pumpkins, cantaloupes, and watermelons too. We also had grapevines, which supplied us with both grape jelly and wine. And there was livestock: chickens, cows, mules, and horses. Even with his brood of children pitching in on planting and harvesting, my father never seemed to get ahead. Regardless of how hard we worked, we had little to show for it, probably because so much of what we grew went to the landowner. We rarely received presents on Christmas, unless my father created homemade items for us. Each of us wore hand-me-downs donated by our cousins, and we all went barefoot, saving the one pair of shoes that each of us had for Sunday and for cold weather. I remember having two pairs of pants; I typically wore one while the other was being washed or mended.

Because we grew our food, we were rarely hungry, but it was still a tough existence. There were chores before and immediately after school, from milking the cows and feeding the livestock to cutting wood for the fires we needed to boil water and cook. Our chores typically meant that we couldn't participate in after-school sports or other activities. I can remember lying in bed on many nights and wondering if this was all there was to life. Even though I'd never ventured beyond our farm and had no idea what options were available to me in the world, I sensed that the life of a sharecropper wouldn't satisfy me. Still, I felt trapped by that same existence.

I know that my father did the very best he could. A deacon at our local Baptist church, I'm sure that his faith helped him through each day. One particular piece of advice he gave me stuck with me throughout my life; I even passed it along to my children. I remember him telling me that however tough we had it, there was always someone having a tougher time. This thought made such an impact on me that I rarely complained after hearing it. Despite being the sole parent, my father managed to raise us well. What he lacked financially he made up for by providing the discipline that all children need. In my case, much of it came in the form of whippings when I violated his strict code. But before he wailed on me with the stick he made me fetch for him, he'd always say, "Son, this will hurt me more than it will hurt you." I wanted to ask him why he'd want to hurt both of us, but I was smart enough to shut my mouth and take my medicine, knowing that this remark would only make matters worse.

While he was stern, my father also demonstrated his love for us in practical ways. Not wanting his children in the care of anyone other than family, he never remarried. The idea of someone else scolding his kids just didn't sit well with him. And despite his heavy workload, he also managed to pay attention to what was going on with each of us. One of the few extracurricular activities I found time to participate in as a youngster was the Boy Scouts. With the loose requirements, I was able to attend local scout meetings without having to invest in a full uniform. Like many of the kids, I got by with just one or two pieces. Attending summer camp, however, required a uniform, something I knew that we couldn't afford. I never asked for the uniform, so I don't know how my father found out that I needed one. Perhaps he heard me talking with my friends, who were excited about the prospect of an entire week at camp. When they asked if I was going, I was too embarrassed to say we couldn't buy the uniform. Instead, I told them that I had important work to do on the farm. My father dealt with the uniform issue in his own way. He didn't say anything to me but found out when the next camp was being held. Then he took on extra work as a groundskeeper at one of the local cemeteries. When he finished the job, he bought my uniform and sent me off to camp. I was probably the proudest, happiest scout there.

While my father's gift of a scout uniform has always been a warm memory, I cannot recall being particularly bothered during my childhood about our lack of material goods. I wasn't aware of any other type of existence, which made it easy for me to accept our situation. As a parent, however, I've probably gone overboard to ensure that my children have never lacked for anything. Once I developed a better understanding of the hard times I experienced, I wanted to spare them the same difficulties.

Growing up in the segregated South during the late 1930s, I came to understand that whites and blacks didn't mix. On public transportation, we were expected to give up our seats to white people. In addition to using separate water fountains and going to separate schools, we were not permitted to try on clothes in stores. Getting served at a restaurant meant going to the back door. These differences became especially apparent to me when my father gave me a quarter for the movies on Saturday afternoons. Even though I walked there with my friend and neighbor Hoyt Stephenson, I had to sit in the balcony while Hoyt sat downstairs. I don't remember questioning this practice, as my father drummed the proper behavior into us at any early age. We knew that we should always call white ladies "miss," even if they were younger than we were. We also had to be certain not to make eye contact with these ladies; we'd tip our hats and count the blocks in the sidewalk until we passed them. Then we could look up again.

Typically, we never entered a white person's home either. If we went there to speak with someone, we were expected to go to the back door and wait. Hoyt's house was the one exception to this rule. His family's religious values taught them that we were all equals. They had no qualms about having me in their home or at their dinner table. It was a special friendship.

My first introduction to law enforcement came when I was twelve years old. My eighteen-year-old brother, Alvin, had a buddy who was caught breaking into the local dry goods store. For some reason, this boy told the sheriff that Alvin had been his accomplice. Even though the storeowner said that nothing was missing and Alvin denied any involvement, he was arrested, charged with robbery, and sentenced to twelve years of labor on a farm owned by the county. Our pastor intervened and convinced the judge to reduce Alvin's sentence to six years.

After serving three years, Alvin was released on probation. He accepted our sister Carrleine's offer to come and stay with her in Norfolk, Virginia, where she and her husband were living. The only problem was that no one told us that he needed permission to leave the state. When we learned that the sheriff had issued a warrant for Alvin's arrest, we contacted Alvin and he promptly returned home, hoping to clear up the confusion. Our father accompanied him to see the sheriff and help to explain. Still, our ignorance of the law was never considered. Alvin spent another two years in prison, and this devastated my father.

Alvin's situation was not uncommon. All of us had heard of other blacks who were arrested simply because the jail needed painting or the county needed a road crew. If you happened to be around when the sheriff was looking for free labor, you might never see the inside of the courthouse; you would simply end up on the chain gang. It was another form of slavery. Years after Alvin served his time, the man who had implicated him told people that my brother had never been involved. Even though the sheriff also learned that Alvin had been framed, nothing ever came of it. Guilt or innocence didn't matter when you were "colored."

Given my early exposure to law enforcement, my eventual career choice is something of a minor miracle. Since we could do nothing about the behavior of the local police, everyone accepted it, even though they weren't much different from the Gestapo agents I'd seen in movies. My familiarity with the ways of the stereotypical southern white sheriff wasn't the only obstacle to my eventual career choice. For a number of years I also had police-related problems in my own family. I was named after my father's brother, Uncle Louie, who came to live with us after he was dismissed from the police force in Washington, D.C. His superiors warned him about the consequences of drinking on the job, but Uncle Louie never straightened out. When he failed to heed these warnings and was fired, he showed up on our doorstep. Sober, he seemed like the nicest man you ever met. After a few drinks, however, his behavior became frightening. He became argumentative, sometimes violent, and wanted to fight everyone. We rarely brought friends home when Uncle Louie was around, as his behavior was so unpredictable. Always protective of his children, my father eventually made his brother find another place to stay.

Being named after Uncle Louie also resulted in confusion. People often think that my name is Louis. It's not Louis, I tell them; it's Louie. I had this discussion with the navy recruiter when I enlisted. He insisted that he had to put me down as Louis. I had to show him my driver's license before he believed me. I'm not certain why I was given the more informal form of this name. Perhaps my parents weren't sure how to spell Louis or maybe giving me the formal version of the name never occurred to them. Since they knew how to spell my uncle's name, they likely went with the familiar version.

Years after the recruiting incident, Uncle Louie's memory came back to haunt me again. When I applied to the Washington, D.C., police department, the interviewer reviewing my background check confused his record with mine and expressed concern about hiring me because of my earlier dismissal for drinking. When I pointed out the birth date of the other Louie McKinney, he realized his error. After we cleared that up, everything went fine.

I don't want to suggest that everything about my childhood was unpleasant. While there were tough times, I also had my share of good experiences for which I'm still thankful. My first celebrity sighting actually occurred in Walhalla. James Brown didn't become widely known until years later, but I first saw him performing in a club near the high school with his group, the Fabulous Flames. He was from a little town in South Carolina called Barnwell, which is about a four-hour drive south of Walhalla.

I didn't think much about James Brown until I became a police officer in Washington, D.C., where I noticed he was performing in the Howard Theater. Since I was working nearby, I walked in while I was in uniform and headed backstage. I told someone working there that I wanted a minute of Mr. Brown's time. The person I spoke with walked back toward a dressing room and I could hear him saying, "A policeman wants to see you."

James Brown didn't sound happy when he replied, "Man, I didn't do nothing! What does he want with me?"

As he walked toward me, I just smiled and said, "Walhalla."

His expression completely changed. "Walhalla! Oh, man, you from Walhalla? Come on in here!"

We talked for quite a while. It actually took a bit of effort for me to get out of there and return to my duties. It amazed me that a celebrity like James Brown was willing to spend so much time with me, a complete stranger, reminiscing about our South Carolina roots.

Growing up on a farm helped me to appreciate hard work. We did more than our share of manual labor on the farm to survive. Those years of hoeing, plowing, shoveling, and chopping wood made a man out of me, blessing me with physical strength that's been an advantage in my chosen field. From an early age, I learned to hunt for possums and other small game. Those days of hunting for food contributed to my skillful marksmanship.

While swimming was never a requirement during my career with the Marshals Service, I've always been a strong swimmer. Because blacks couldn't swim in the public pools, my schoolmates and I made our own swimming hole by damming up the local creek. I always won the little contests we held to see who could hold their breath the longest. My confidence in the water helped me to save Hoyt, who got into trouble once while we were swimming. One hot day Hoyt jumped into the swimming hole to cool off, even though he had never learned to swim. Seeing him flailing around helplessly, I made the mistake of approaching him from the front, something lifesaving courses warn against. In his panic, he nearly drowned both of us. After I pushed him away, I had the sense to grab him from behind and pull him to safety.

More than once I found myself in harm's way at this creek. When I was younger, my father frequently warned me to stay away from one section of the creek where some beavers were building a dam. Fascinated by the beavers' agility in the water, I couldn't bring myself to obey him. When my father was busy working, I'd sneak down to the creek to observe the animals. As I stood on the bank watching one day, I kept changing my position to get a better look. After moving to one spot, something told me to look down. At my feet was a water moccasin, curled and ready to strike. Screaming, I ran into the water, across the creek, and straight up the opposite bank. Frightened by the snake, I later told my father what had happened. I'd rather face a hundred whippings than go anywhere near a snake.

Even though I may have disappointed my father that day by going where I was not supposed to go, my performance in school was never a cause for concern. Together with my natural curiosity came an ability to remember anything we were taught, which made me a straight-A student. When we were excused from school for most of September to help with the harvest, I always caught up quickly. Teachers frequently told me, "One day you're going to be somebody, Louie." Their encouraging words never sunk in. I'd look at them puzzled. My limited perspective told me that I'd never be anything but a farmer.

I wasn't opposed to cutting class, especially if I had a chance to work. I never stole anything, not even a watermelon. I always worked to pay for what I wanted. Even though I frequently risked being caught by the truant officer, school just couldn't compare to making money.

As soon as I was old enough, I began taking odd jobs in addition to my regular chores. I'd make pocket money by pumping gas or washing dishes at local restaurants. One of my earliest jobs involved cutting grass at Clemson University, where I was paid the princely sum of fifty cents a day. Along with one or two other boys, I'd ride in the back of the truck that came through town to take us to the university grounds, about sixteen miles away.

The campus seemed enormous. Once we finished pushing the mowers, it was time to start over again. We didn't use power mowers either; we were the ones supplying the power to spin the mowers' rotary blades. After we cut a section of grass, we'd rake the clippings into piles. At lunchtime, we'd go to the kitchen's back door, where the lady doing the cooking gave us food. It was tedious work, but I was always glad to get paid.

My father, who would allow me time off from the farmwork for the day, always encouraged my moonlighting efforts. "Son," he'd say, "working keeps your mind busy. You'll stay out of trouble that way."

Like most boys, I was prone to mischief. I'd play tricks on kids at school, and they would get even. These exchanges are common with all children, and the details are long forgotten. However, I've never forgotten how one young colt taught me the consequences of teasing an animal when I was about eleven years old. For some time I was bothered because this beautiful horse wouldn't let me ride him. Even though I was a good rider, every time I'd get on his back, he'd throw me. Deciding to repay him, I waited until he was in his stall, unable to move. Then I put a feedbag on his back where he couldn't reach it. Smelling the oats and being unable to get them drove him crazy, and he began kicking and making a ruckus. Sometimes I'd even touch him with a pitchfork. I wouldn't pierce his skin; I just wanted him to feel the points.

Animals never forget such teasing; this smart horse simply waited for the right moment. One day, as we were putting the mules in the pasture where this horse was grazing, I slipped and fell. The horse, which I had just shooed down the hill to let the mules in, saw his opportunity. As I tried to get up, he came after me. Luckily, my uncle chased him off just as he reared back to strike me with his hooves. I never bothered that horse again.

My curiosity and my desire to make a better life for myself reached a breaking point when I was fourteen. For some time I'd instinctively known that life on the farm was a dead end for me. Since I'd never been out of Walhalla, I lacked direction. A postcard from my cousin provided the encouragement that I needed. "Come on up, Louie," wrote Robert, who had moved from nearby Westminster to New Jersey to be with his girlfriend. "You'll love it in Asbury Park. It's right on the ocean and you'll have no problem finding work."

The idea of changing my life by going somewhere new grew more and more enticing. While I couldn't stop thinking about it, I never told a soul about Robert's invitation; I especially avoided saying anything to my father. One day, without a word to anyone, I impulsively followed my cousin's travel instructions by walking down the road and putting out my thumb. My first ride took me to Washington, D.C. From there, a sailor picked me up and drove me all the way to my destination. He even dropped me off on the corner of Springwood Avenue, which was where Robert lived.

When I learned that Robert and his girlfriend didn't have room for me at their place, I wasn't discouraged. Instead, I got a room at the local YMCA, and Robert took me on a tour of the local sights, including the beach and the boardwalk. Things were different in New Jersey. In Asbury Park, I had my first encounter with indoor plumbing. On the farm, we used an outhouse, a place where I never felt completely comfortable, especially on cold mornings. Still, I was shocked at the sight of indoor accommodations.

A bigger shock awaited me. Wanting to continue my education, I asked Robert to point me toward the nearest school. When he took me to Asbury Park High School on Sunset Avenue, I thought he'd made a mistake.

"Wait a minute, this can't be the right place," I said, as I watched the white students walking by.

Robert insisted that this was the only school around, but I resisted. "Robert, you know I can't go here," I said, a bit upset. "Take me to the black school."

Smiling, Robert told me that there were no black schools, that the schools in New Jersey were integrated. Unaccustomed to being around so many white people, but wanting to continue learning, I enrolled. When the results of my placement test came back, I found that I would go into the tenth grade and skip the ninth grade entirely. I wasn't completely convinced that skipping a grade was the best idea, but I didn't say anything. In the end, having more challenging work to do probably kept me from getting bored.

Still, I was scared about this new environment and became increasingly uncomfortable when people laughed at my southern accent. When I discovered that my assigned seat was right next to a white girl, I nearly fled the school in a panic. The double seats used in schools back then put us side by side, which was much too close for me. I was petrified. I kept my hands folded for fear of touching her and never ventured to talk to her or look in her direction. In a segregated culture, my behavior would have been fine. In an integrated school, it regularly caused my seatmate to ask me what was wrong. She must have thought that I was crazy. It would take quite a while for me to become comfortable in an integrated world.

As Robert had promised, I had no problem finding work. I swept the floors in a local barbershop, set pins in the bowling alley on the boardwalk, and took any other jobs that I could find. Frequently I'd get work in Deal, an adjacent town, where I'd be paid fifty cents a day for raking leaves. When my math teacher, Mrs. Law, learned that I was on my own, she began taking an interest in me by giving me work at her home, which was also in Deal. For some time I did her yard work and performed various chores around her house, from cleaning windows to sweeping floors. In addition to paying me, she always fed me well whenever I worked. Sometimes she would give me clothes that her grown children had worn when they were young.

During the months that I was in New Jersey, I never contacted my family. It pains me now to think about how my disappearance must have affected my father. When my friend Ken Chapman replied to a postcard I sent him, I learned that my father had the sheriff looking for me. I told Ken not to tell anyone where I was. To this day, I regret my impetuous decision to leave home. The effect of my actions never really sunk in until I had children of my own.

Just as suddenly as I had departed, I decided to return, and hitchhiked home to Walhalla. After months of not seeing my father or my family, I wasn't sure how I would be received. I truly expected a whipping. Instead, it was like the biblical story about the prodigal son. My father smiled, hugged my neck, and with tears in his eyes, told me he was glad that I was home.

Asbury Park was only the beginning of my travels. Together with Hoyt, I began talking seriously about joining the navy. We decided that we'd enlist together. Because I was underage, I needed my dad's signature to sign up. Even though I'm sure that he didn't want me to leave again, he didn't try to talk me out of it. He talked with me man to man, trying to ensure that enlisting was what I really wanted.

The navy had a program known as the Kiddie Cruise that had attracted me and Hoyt. It allowed a seventeen-year-old boy to enlist and be released before his twenty-first birthday. With my dad's permission, I headed off to the recruiting station that was set up once a week by the local Selective Service Board, only to have the recruiter send me home for proof of age. Because there was no Bureau of Vital Statistics that held black families' birth records, I went to the family Bible, which listed all this important information. When

I did the math, however, I was disappointed to discover that I was still only sixteen and had to wait nearly a year.

My desire to get away continued to grow, as I felt that I was wasting away on the farm. Unable to tolerate school any longer because I wanted to be in the navy, I dropped out in the eleventh grade. When I turned seventeen, I immediately returned to the recruiting station. There were other obstacles to overcome this time, including taking aptitude tests and physicals. Although I passed the entrance exam with flying colors, the recruiter was suspicious of my high grade and forced me to retake it. The second time I scored even higher. Traveling to Columbia, South Carolina, for the physical brought yet another disappointment. While Hoyt passed, I was turned down because I was underweight. Knowing the physical work that I was capable of, the verdict puzzled me. Hoyt went off to boot camp, while I returned home to eat bananas, potatoes, and anything else I thought would put on the necessary pounds. It took three trips, but I finally made weight and was accepted.

My satisfaction was short-lived. While I was supposed to head directly to the Naval Training Center in Great Lakes, Illinois, I had a strange urge to return home first. As I neared the farm, eager to tell my family the good news, I saw that my sisters were gathered outside the house crying. With a sinking feeling in my stomach, I thought that we'd lost one of my younger sisters who had been sick for a while. But it wasn't my sister who had died; it was my father. I found his passing very difficult to accept and struggled with guilt, feeling that he'd still be alive if I hadn't run away. It took a long time for me to accept that he died because he had heart problems, that it had nothing to do with me. In our little town, my father was very well respected. More white people than black people attended his funeral, something that was unheard of in those days. Still, at fifty-five years old, he was a fairly young man when he passed.

Because we couldn't afford to keep running the farm and paying the bills, we had to part with our home. Even though it was a difficult period, we took the time to care for each other. While some of my siblings went to live with our cousins, everyone encouraged me to pursue my dream of entering the navy. With my family's blessing behind me, I headed off to boot camp.

The navy was the start of many good things for me. It launched what would become a lifelong love affair with traveling. The first hint of my inclination for these voyages wasn't my trip to Asbury Park. It was a brief conversation with a local Native-American medicine man that occurred when I was eight years old. After examining my palm, the medicine man said that I had a "traveling hand," which meant that I would have many enjoyable journeys throughout my life.

For a country boy, the twelve-hour train ride from rural South Carolina to Chicago was an event in itself. I was so excited that I barely slept. Thanks to the meal coupons the recruiter gave me, I ate well. I'd never seen anything like the crowds that I witnessed when I arrived in Chicago. I marveled at the subways and the tall buildings, struck by how different the city was from my little farm town. When I attended my specialty training school after boot camp, I returned frequently to Chicago to take in the sights. I was thrilled when the navy's service center gave us tickets to see Sarah Vaughn, one of my favorite singers. Sitting in that theater and hearing her performance gave me goose bumps. I couldn't believe what great things were happening to me.

When I enlisted, a waiting period of six months to a year stood between me and my goal of becoming a sailor. Unwilling to wait any longer, I accepted the only way around this obstacle, which involved signing on as a steward. This meant that I spent the early years of my naval career working in galleys, cooking, and learning to care for an officer's stateroom and uniforms. After completing the specialty school for stewards, I was assigned to the Naval Academy in Annapolis. Although I could barely pronounce Annapolis and had never heard of the academy, when I saw it, I thought it was the most beautiful place that I'd ever seen. The combination of the historic town set on the Chesapeake Bay, the campus, and the midshipmen in their uniforms seemed like something out of a picture book.

Since the majority of the stewards were black, we were housed on a barge in the bay. It was referred to disparagingly as the "African Queen," but it was a floating hotel that had everything we needed. In the morning we'd march to Bancroft Hall to set the tables, prepare the food, and clean up. We'd march back to the barge in the evening when our work was finished. I was assigned to a crew for a few days and then had a few days off to see the sights and go to the beach with the other enlisted men. I fell in love with Annapolis back in my early navy days; it's no surprise that I eventually chose to make the town my home.

The navy gave me great opportunities to travel, exposing me to a wealth of new places and experiences. I saw cities and countries that I never would have been able to visit. While I was seeing all of this, I was working and getting paid, as well as being fed, clothed, and housed.

Eager to fulfill my dream of sailing the seas, I volunteered for the summer midshipmen's cruise, which put me on the ocean for twenty-one days. I watched the ship approaching from across the bay, excited that I'd soon be aboard and headed overseas. Whenever I wasn't working, I was up on the deck hanging over the rails and staring into the horizon.

The first port that I saw was La Caruña, Spain, where the townspeople lit fires in the street to welcome the ship as we docked. Even though I was a bit uncomfortable aboard a ship of mostly white sailors, my race rarely was an issue. After a while, I began to enjoy visiting the churches, museums, and local bars with my shipmates. We had a good time, dancing and drinking Spanish wine.

From Spain, we journeyed to Antwerp, Belgium. Again, the local people seemed to welcome us. I spent many nights sitting in the local bars buying drinks and enjoying conversations, especially the conversations with the ladies. However, not everyone was happy about a black sailor talking with a white woman. One of my shipmates, who seemed to be having problems with my socializing, asked me to go outside and talk with him. When I did, he surprised me by immediately punching me in the face. When the Shore Patrol arrived to break up the fight, they locked me up, thinking that I'd started it. Given my earlier youthful tendencies, it was a bit ironic. Thankfully, there were no hard feelings. The other sailor, who was much bigger than I was, was amazed at my strength. "You sure gave me a whipping," he confessed. The two of us became quite friendly.

After the cruise, we returned to Annapolis and I resumed my duties at the Naval Academy. While visiting the local beach on one of my days off, I met a young woman from Baltimore and we began dating. After seeing each other for about a year, we were married in March 1954.

I put in another eighteen months at the academy before I was reassigned to Long Beach, California. I had requested this tour because I'd always dreamed of seeing California. Because my new ship was in Japan, I was told that I would be sent to the naval receiving station in San Francisco for two weeks to await transportation. During this time, my wife went to stay with her mother in Baltimore until I returned.

The trip to California far exceeded my expectations. After an enjoyable time of wandering around Fisherman's Wharf, looking across the bay at Alcatraz Island, and taking in the other sights, I boarded a plane to Japan that stopped in Hawaii for a few days. I had such a good time visiting the local bars with the other sailors who were also heading to Japan that I missed my flight. They tried in vain to wake me after our last night of celebrating. When I woke up alone in the barracks where we were temporarily housed, I worried that I would be court-martialed. Instead, I was simply put on a bus to the naval air station on the other side of the island to catch another transport. When we stopped in Guam to refuel, I behaved myself this time.

We landed in Tokyo, and I went directly to the naval station in Yokosuka, where I was assigned to a troop transport. It was smaller than the cruiser that I'd been on with the midshipmen, with fewer stewards and fewer officers, but it was a great assignment. We completed a number of runs between Japan and California, and I always enjoyed the various ports I visited, as well as our stops in the Philippines. Each new city was an education. I soaked up the local culture, the sights, and the people.

In Sasebo, Japan, I got a little too close to the local culture. One day we were riding bicycles through the country when my hat flew off. I stopped my bike to retrieve my hat, which had flown into a round pit. As I walked toward it, a couple of Japanese farmers stood nearby, waving their arms at me and saying what sounded like, "Benji, benji!" I had no idea what they were saying and continued retrieving my hat, despite the awful smell. I later learned that my hat landed in an outdoor toilet, called a benji. For the next six months many of my shipmates called me "benji" and some other foul names.

Traveling wasn't the only benefit of my naval career. The navy nourished and encouraged my love for learning. There wasn't much to do at sea after my twelve-hour shift ended, so I spent much of my time reading and studying. I took every class that our training officers provided. I enrolled in GED classes and earned my high school equivalency, took college-level courses in history and literature, and successfully followed the difficult path of becoming a radio operator. I even accomplished this without taking any classes at the stateside school that other radio operators attended. As a radio operator, I went on assignments in the South Pole, completed two tours in the Mediterranean, and served at the Commander, Military Sea Transportation Service (COMSTS) in Washington, D.C.

The navy changed everything for me. When my enlistment ended while I was serving in Long Beach in 1957, I wisely chose to reenlist. While the signing bonus was attractive, I instinctively knew that I was getting much more than that. I was gaining the discipline and direction that I needed to succeed in life.

For a country boy who rarely ventured anywhere, who went to bed when the sun went down and rose as soon as it came up again, the navy was like a dream come true. Somehow the navy even managed to put me in the right place at the right time, the place where I'd take the next step in my career.

Close to my discharge date in 1963, I was in Washington, D.C., walking down Wisconsin Avenue near the COMSTS building where I worked. I saw a sign on a passing transit bus. "Wanted. Police officers," it read. I had no idea what good things were still ahead. One door was closing, but another one was opening.

3
Tales of Two Badges
The D.C. Metropolitan Police Department and
the U.S. Marshals Service

I was enduring yet another long, boring day as a new deputy U.S. marshal.
Six days a week I reported to the U.S. Marshals office inside the federal
court building in Washington, D.C. Like every federal court in the country,
the courthouse on Indiana Avenue has space for the marshals that includes a
cellblock capable of holding up to thirty prisoners. From seven in the morning
until six at night, I brought prisoners upstairs before the judges for sentencing
and then back downstairs to these holding cells.

The only thing worse than moving prisoners was the waiting. Sentencing
is typically a lengthy process; it's not uncommon for one case to take up to
two hours. Often the sheer backlog of cases on the docket is enough to cause
delays. If a judge entertains motions from an attorney or a lawyer arrives late
from another case, the time drags. Typically, once we brought a prisoner into
a courtroom, we couldn't leave while the judge was present. Our presence
ensured that the prisoners wouldn't hurt anyone or disrupt the court. We were
also there to restrain prisoners who might react to a sentence they perceived
as too lengthy or unfair.

On their best days, prisoners in handcuffs and leg irons were difficult people to be with. They were surly and prone to frequently cursing us and calling
us pigs. On days when they were awaiting sentencing, they seemed even more
ornery than usual. Once they stood before the judge, however, they generally
calmed down. At other times, there were few prisoners for me to move. On

those days I sat in the marshals' office near the holding block, making sure that the few prisoners we had didn't hurt themselves or each other.

This monotony was interrupted only by the process-serving duties. Since the Marshals Service was initially formed to serve the federal courts, I went to homes on nearly a daily basis to deliver the subpoenas, indictments, and other papers notifying people of court appearances. And since the marshals are responsible for the duties normally performed by a sheriff within the District of Columbia, I delivered eviction notices and other court documents. It was another thankless job, one that was made worse by the many people who became upset when I showed up with these papers.

Every day I was feeling less like a deputy marshal and more like a bailiff or a messenger. To worsen matters, I didn't even have a badge. Back then the Marshals Service didn't often have new badges made. After being sworn in as a deputy U.S. marshal in March 1968, I was given a paper certificate and told that I would get a badge when another deputy retired. After six or seven months of this tedious work, I'd reached the end of my rope. I couldn't believe that I'd left my exciting job at the D.C. Metropolitan Police Department for this grunt work.

Prompted by a sign that I saw on the back of a passing bus, I joined the police department in Washington, D.C., in 1963, immediately after leaving the navy, and took to the work right away. After filling out the application and passing the background investigation and the aptitude test, I was assigned to the sixth precinct. In those days rookie officers were often trained by being paired with veterans. My partner, Ed Warren, gave me an education that I wouldn't have received anywhere else. He showed me how to detect a stolen car by seeing if its tag numbers had been altered or the driver was behaving nervously. I also learned not to enter a bank right after it opened or right before it closed, since that was when most robberies occurred. Ed also taught me how to protect myself when checking alleys, which meant staying out of the shadows where I could be attacked. Using a flashlight safely involved holding it to the side, since anyone trying to shoot you will typically aim at the beam. It was valuable on-the-job training.

Periodically, the sergeant came by to observe me. After I had spent a few months walking the beat with Ed, the sergeant took a turn working with me for two weeks and asked me many questions about police procedures. When we walked past parked cars, he quizzed me to see if I noticed any parking violations. He observed me closely while I wrote tickets to see how I handled myself. He also expected me to be able to estimate how fast a passing car was going, as well as to remain aware of the many things that were going on around us. When he was satisfied by my answers and performance, he simply told me that I was ready to walk a beat by myself. I was surprised. There were other rookies who had been training with senior officers for a year, so it was quite a compliment. I was glad that I had graduated.

Every day that I was at the precinct, I enjoyed putting on my uniform and badge. It didn't matter that my newcomer status got me assigned to walking a beat in warehouse districts where little happened and there was nowhere to eat or get coffee. It didn't matter when a lieutenant made it abundantly clear that no colored officers would be assigned to patrol cars. It didn't matter that the white officers didn't want me riding with them. I loved being a police officer; it was in my blood. One night I got the opportunity to prove myself.

I was working the graveyard shift from midnight to eight in the morning on this particular Saturday. Since there weren't enough officers to fill the patrol cars, I was assigned to one. My white partner initially protested our pairing. Since a car could not go out with only one officer, there was little he could do about it. Except for stressing that he didn't want me falling asleep in the car, he maintained an angry silence. At 2:00 a.m. we received a call that an officer was in trouble in a nearby precinct. When we arrived at the scene, I saw four or five black men beating the officer. I jumped out of the car, swung my nightstick at them, and then pulled the perpetrators away from the downed patrolman.

When we returned to the station, my partner began telling everyone that I went against some of my own people to protect a white officer. I quickly interrupted him. "It had nothing to do with what color anybody was," I said. "The man who was on the ground was a brother officer in trouble. It's my duty to help him." My devotion to the job broke whatever barriers existed in the precinct. I had proved myself under pressure. In the eyes of my fellow officers, I had earned my badge.

While my five years with the D.C. Metropolitan Police were satisfying, my new role with the Marshals Service wasn't turning out to be what I'd expected. In frustration, I spoke with my former sergeant at the sixth precinct. He assured me that he would be happy to take me back; I was glad that I could be a police officer again. In the months that I'd been a deputy, I'd seen nothing of the intrigue or excitement that first attracted me to the Marshals Service. There was no evidence of the thrilling life that I'd sensed when talking with Joe Crown.

Since I knew how to type from my navy days, I frequently worked in the police stationhouse as a desk sergeant. There, I communicated with the cars by radio, typed up police reports, and handled the paperwork for arrests. On many mornings a sharply dressed man would come into the precinct with a prisoner. In his three-piece suit and hat, he impressed me as a modern-day Bat Masterson, the legendary frontier lawman who was frequently portrayed as a stylish dresser. The way this modern lawman carried himself communicated that he was someone to reckon with. His name was Joe Crown, and he was the first deputy U.S. marshal I'd ever met.

Joe was bringing in fugitives on a regular basis. With warrants from the U.S. District Court in hand, he tracked down these wanted men, rousting them early in the morning when they were less likely to cause trouble. It wasn't uncommon for Joe to find these men in a stupor after a night of wasting themselves on booze, drugs, or both. Even if they weren't wasted, it wouldn't have mattered. At six foot two, Joe was trim, muscular, and confident. He looked like someone who would handle himself well during a confrontation.

When I asked him where his backup was, Joe just smiled at me and found a unique way to communicate that he didn't need any. "One riot, one marshal," he said, as he led his prisoner toward the cell. I knew that Joe was modifying the expression, "One riot, one ranger," typically associated with the Texas Rangers. Somehow, when he said it, it seemed fitting.

My curiosity aroused, I began reading about the Marshals Service and asking Joe questions whenever he showed up at the station. I'd heard of Wyatt Earp and had seen deputy marshals in Westerns, but had no idea that the service still existed. As I read more about it, I learned that the U.S. Marshals Service was the very first federal law-enforcement agency.

What most drew me to the Marshals Service was what happened in 1962. The U.S. Marshals had been the force that integrated the University of Mississippi by enabling a black student named James Meredith to attend classes. The marshals distinguished themselves by enduring attacks by irate southerners who rioted on the campus to protest Meredith's presence. Despite being outnumbered and having many injured deputies, they refused to back down.

The more that I learned about the Marshals, the more I was attracted to the service. I decided to find out how I could become a deputy. Joining the Marshals Service required passing a Treasury Department test. On a day off I rode a cab down to the Office of Personnel Management on Eighteenth Street to take the next scheduled examination, which involved certain aptitude tests. A month later I was notified that I'd passed, and then I underwent a background investigation and a psychiatric evaluation, which I also passed. Excited, I eagerly awaited a call from the Marshals Service about how I'd begin this promising new career.

The Bureau of Alcohol, Tobacco, and Firearms was the first agency to contact me and offer me an opportunity to become an agent. Since I'd taken a Treasury Department test, ATF had also been notified of my passing grade. Even though I politely declined, the agency pressed me a bit. The man asked, "Are you sure that you don't want to become an ATF agent?" "No," I said firmly, "I want to be a marshal." Thanking him again for the offer, I hung up the phone.

Months passed. Close to midnight on March 5, 1967, as I was getting ready for bed, I heard the phone ringing. "Who'd be calling at this hour?" I wondered.

"My name is Luke Moore," the voice on the phone said. "I'm a United States marshal." Thinking it was a prank call, I hung up. No marshal would call at this hour, I thought.

As I walked away, the phone rang another time. Again, the caller identified himself as Luke Moore. Sometime later I learned that Luke was the
second African American ever appointed by the president as a U.S. marshal.
The first was famed abolitionist Frederick Douglass, who was appointed by
President Rutherford B. Hayes in 1877. Luke was a trailblazer, accomplish-
ing things that were rare among African Americans at the time. He went on
to become a U.S. attorney and a respected federal judge. I also learned that
these late-night phone calls were standard procedure for him, as he frequently worked past normal hours.

Getting right to the point, Luke asked if I still wanted to become a deputy
marshal, as so much time had passed since I'd taken the exam. When I said
that I did, he asked me to come to his office at nine o'clock in the morning.
After interviewing me that day, Luke asked when I could start. We discussed
how much notice the police department needed and agreed on a tentative date.

Two weeks later, when I had to turn in my gun and badge at the precinct,
it was difficult to say good-bye to my fellow officers. I felt very emotional, like
I was leaving part of myself behind. It took some self-control not to cry.

Once I had joined the Marshals Service, however, I felt torn. The thought
of returning to my old precinct and wearing the uniform and badge was appealing. Still, I wasn't quite ready to abandon the dream of being like Joe
Crown. I wanted to apprehend fugitives, bust down doors, and rid the streets
of dangerous criminals. Instead, I was spending day after day in district court,
escorting prisoners between the courtroom and their cells. I knew that wasn't
what I wanted to do.

Just as I was about to resign, after working for the Marshals Service for
nearly six months, another phone call changed everything for me. This one
came in the afternoon, and the caller's name was Ellis Duley. A deputy U.S.
marshal, he was in charge of wrangling together the district's new warrant
squad. He'd learned that I'd been a police officer and wondered if I'd be interested in joining this unit. He thought that my police experience prepared me
for doing the investigative work needed to help apprehend bail jumpers, people who had violated parole, or those who had escaped from federal prison.
Since there were many of these violators, the judges wanted something done

to get them off the streets. Because of our connection to the courts, finding them was the responsibility of the Marshals Service. Within our district, our new unit would assume this work as a full-time job.

While I was happy to be moving to more exciting duties, at the time I was somewhat ignorant of how my work in the federal courts fit within the larger mission of the Marshals Service. I was focused only on becoming like Joe Crown. While apprehending fugitives is an important part of the service's work, so is working with the federal courts. The Marshals Service and the federal courts have always been linked. When the First Continental Congress created the court system, it also created the Marshals Service to enforce federal law. The president appointed marshals in each of the country's ninety-four judicial districts. One additional position was also created in the District of Columbia, giving the nation ninety-five U.S. marshals.

Today, the service protects thousands of federal judges and courthouses across the country, providing security during high-risk trials, as well as designing the security systems for federal court buildings. Marshals also oversee the work of the court security officers who were later contracted by the Marshals Service to perform the jobs that I handled early in my career. Having court security officers has freed our deputies to perform more essential duties.

I've always thought that "The Silent Service" was a good description of the U.S. Marshals. Much of what we did was rarely publicized because we lacked a public information office for some years. While most people have heard of Elliot Ness and J. Edgar Hoover, not many know about other federal agents who made history in their own quiet way.

When I joined the warrant squad in Washington, D.C., in 1968, I had the privilege of working for many of the modern-day legends of the Marshals Service. Men such as Carlton Beall, Al Butler, Ellis Duley, Donald Forsht, Harvey Madley, and Frank Vandergrift began revolutionizing the Marshals Service. Their dedication, teamwork, and professionalism gained the service respect and recognition from the Justice Department, the public, and the law-enforcement community.

The U.S. Marshals' former historian Frederick Calhoun described the importance of what these men accomplished. "Butler, Forsht, and the others were mavericks at a tumultuous time. Together, they changed the history of the marshals and, in no small part, the history of the United States."[1]

Before these men became marshals, a few people like Joe Crown went after fugitives, but they were able to do this work only on an occasional basis. Most marshals regarded working with the courts as our number-one responsibility; fugitive apprehensions and other details were considered only after we were done taking prisoners to the courtroom and finished our process-serving duties. The warrant squad that Ellis Duley organized in Washington, D.C., changed that thinking dramatically. In a few years the operation that began in our district became the model that was adopted by every one of the service's ninety-four districts. Across the country, deputies would be committed full-time to the job of catching fugitives.

Ellis Duley—the man who brought me into the warrant squad—was a good person to work for. An even-tempered guy, he simply told you what had to be done and expected you to do it. Even though he was the chief of the warrant squad, he was very understanding and let you do things your way. He wasn't a micromanager. If you messed up, he'd call you in, chew you out, and tell you not to let it happen again. Unlike a lot of people in government jobs, he was flexible. As long as you got things done, it was fine if you had to come in late or leave early. He understood that sometimes people had to take care of other responsibilities.

Ellis reported to Al Butler, who was the chief deputy. A chief deputy is the highest position that a deputy can hold, outside of being one of the ninety-five marshals appointed by the president. This person is typically the marshal's second in command.

I can't say enough about Al Butler. My boss for many years, he managed to be a tough, no-nonsense individual and a real people-oriented person. That's a pretty amazing combination, but Al was an amazing guy. He made sure that deserving people were promoted, ensured that important work was ef-

---

1. Frederick S. Calhoun, *The Lawmen: United States Marshals and Their Deputies, 1789–1989* (New York: Penguin Books, 1991), 258.

ficiently organized, and got the equipment we needed to get our work done. The service knew how valuable Al's contributions were and eventually President Nixon's administration appointed him as the marshal for the state of Maryland in 1970.

Al was very tough, a real cop. If there was trouble, he was the man that you'd want on your side. There's a story in Calhoun's *The Lawmen* about his interview for his first job with the Marshals Service. The marshal interviewing him was a little nervous about Al's reputation as a fighter. Al told him, "I never hit a man in my life that didn't ripple his muscles at me first."[2] A few years later, when I was in training to join the service's elite Special Operations Group, I wasn't surprised that Al was one of our self-defense instructors. When I became acting director of the service, Al was retiring. It was a privilege for me to make sure that he received his credentials as a retired U.S. marshal.

Frank Vandergrift was our assistant chief. Like the roll-call sergeant in the police department, he worked the squad room, making assignments. Frank came from a military family; his father had been a high-ranking Marine. Frank, who had majored in business administration in college, was a capable and gifted administrator who could efficiently handle paperwork that would get many people bogged down and frustrated. When the Witness Protection Program needed help organizing its administrative operations a few years later, I knew that Frank would be a perfect person for that position. And he was.

Carlton Beall, who was the marshal for the District of Columbia at the time, brought in every one of these impressive deputies. Beall had been the sheriff for Prince Georges County in Maryland and knew these men from their police work in that department. He deserves a lot of credit for building a team that began slowly turning things around for the Marshals Service. And turning the Marshals around was becoming more and more of a necessity.

Once the frontier marshals disappeared with the Wild West, the Marshals Service didn't have the best reputation. Being appointed a marshal in any of the country's judicial districts was seen as little more than political patronage; many of the appointed marshals even lacked basic law-enforcement experience.

---

2.   Calhoun, *The Lawmen*, 258.

As a result, the overall organization lacked focus and was overlooked within the Justice Department. It was nearly impossible for the Marshals Service to be considered an equal with specialized, well-funded federal agencies like the FBI, the Secret Service, and others. In *The Lawmen*, Calhoun writes, "Officials viewed the marshals as archaic holdovers from the frontier. No one quite knew what to do with them in a modern world."[3]

Sadly, deputy marshals were perceived as little more than the fat bailiffs working in courtrooms and jails. Since the districts were typically short-staffed, deputies did little more than serve the courts, just as I did early in my career. Most deputies rarely had any opportunity to exercise the broad arrest powers that came from the service's association with the federal courts. By contrast, FBI agents had no arrest powers in the bureau's early years. After their agents conducted an investigation, they depended on the Marshals Service to make the necessary arrests. Somehow everyone seemed to have forgotten who the marshals were. During my time with the warrant squad, this energetic team of young men began to change that muddled understanding.

Instead of contributing to that tarnished image, the deputies on the warrant squad began exercising their authority. They weren't content to sit around the courts. They began acting like investigators and hunting down wanted fugitives. Once they started that ball rolling, the rest of the service began acting differently. In time, every district across the country copied the idea and began launching warrant squads. These men really were a different breed.

Another reason that things began changing was the Marshals Service's new leadership. Jim McShane, a former Golden Gloves boxer and New York homicide detective, met Robert Kennedy while serving as part-time chauffer for Kennedy's in-laws. Impressed by McShane, Robert convinced him to join his Senate racketeering staff and later made him chief of security during his brother's presidential campaign. When John Kennedy became president in 1960, Robert became attorney general and appointed Jim McShane to head the Marshals Service.

---

3. Calhoun, *The Lawmen*, 255.

As the chief U.S. marshal, McShane expanded the role of the service's Executive Office beyond its focus on bureaucratic paperwork. This move began a slow transformation by providing the service with a central point for organizing our operations. Prior to McShane's leadership, there wasn't a centralized hub for the entire service—only independent districts that did whatever that local marshal decided. Since the president appointed each district's marshal and the Executive Office answered to the deputy attorney general, the tug-of-war between the local marshals and this centralized organization was understandable. McShane's connections with the Kennedy brothers overcame some of this resistance and enabled the service to increase its professionalism. For example, when civil service hiring standards were implemented, the local marshals no longer had complete control over the hiring of their deputies.

When Butler, Duley, and Donald Forsht organized the first in-depth training for deputies, professional standards were raised further. Prior to this, the service offered limited on-the-job training, a strategy that worked only when hiring candidates with previous police experience. The two-week training sessions they designed were modeled after the Treasury Department's comprehensive curriculum. I was one of the first deputies to go through that training, which was a pilot to determine if it could be successful. The training was a mix of classroom education and practical techniques. It schooled new deputies in investigative tactics, search and seizure methods, making arrests, courtroom procedures, and testifying in court. It also offered training in making car stops, handcuffing, the use of a nightstick, and karate.

Today's training is even more rigorous and well defined. Deputies must meet strict fitness standards for running, push-ups, and sit-ups. There are also firearm qualification standards. Deputies are prepared to perform increasingly specialized duties. By the time they graduate from the Federal Law Enforcement Training Center in Glynco, Georgia, they are well versed in investigative techniques. They have learned how to check records and use data to pinpoint a fugitive's trail. They have also been trained in basic protective services, which will enable them to safeguard government witnesses, as well as protect visiting foreign dignitaries.

Jim McShane's reputation as a tough, Irish cop who wouldn't back down from anyone or anything led the Kennedy administration to depend on him for a critical mission: They wanted the Marshals Service to enforce the desegregation of the South. McShane, Duley, Butler, Vandergrift, and many of the other men with whom I served had been part of the small squad of marshals that protected James Meredith and endured the ensuing riots. They also made sure that a six-year-old African-American girl named Ruby Bridges could attend the all-white William Frantz Public School in New Orleans in 1960. Integrating the South and experiencing racial segregation was an experience that forever changed them. It also increased the positive public recognition of the Marshals Service for the first time in many years.

Because Beall had brought some of these deputies with him from the sheriff's department, they were called his "good ole boys." But there was never a hint of prejudice from any of them. I was never treated any differently from the other deputies; everyone was treated with the same respect.

As one of thirty deputies in the warrant squad, I helped to track down bail jumpers and parole violators across Washington, D.C., Virginia, and Maryland. Typically, the courts wanted these people because they didn't show up for arraignment after posting bail.

When they failed to appear in court, arrest warrants were generated. Frequently we'd get a bundle of active warrants, which enabled the court to purge its files. We would execute the warrants and get the violators off the streets. Since many of them were repeat offenders, it was important to find them. Finding fugitives involves using standard investigative tools. Using court records, we typically started with the last known address and began questioning relatives, friends, and neighbors. When necessary, we checked IRS tax records, telephone company records, and motor vehicle databases. It's not uncommon to find many fugitives still living at their last known addresses.

If we had an arrest warrant for a parole violator, we'd bring him straight to jail. If he had posted bond and failed to appear, we would take him before the nearest magistrate and have him arraigned. The judge would then decide how to deal with him.

Washington, D.C., is somewhat different from other parts of the country.

There, the marshals also covered the work normally handled by the county sheriff. That meant that in addition to executing federal warrants from the district court, we worked the warrants for the superior court. This additional duty provided another reason that a full-time warrant squad was needed in the area.

Like Joe Crown, we started very early in the morning, around 5:30 or 6:00 a.m. We'd obtain violators' previous addresses from court records and apprehend them early, usually while they were still sleeping. Most of the time, they weren't hard to deal with. I participated in countless raids and don't recall many people giving us a hard time. Very few tried to fight or even to run away. Once in a while, someone would pretend that he was not the person that we were trying to find. Often violators would proclaim their innocence, projecting their guilt onto someone else. Nobody wants to be arrested.

Of course we frequently had the element of surprise on our side. Imagine for a moment that several armed marshals arrived at your home early in the morning. They came through the front door and the back door, all the while yelling, "Federal officers! Put your hands where I can see them." Chances are that you'd do what you were told.

At the time I was in my late twenties. While I understood that executing a warrant could evolve into a dangerous situation, I don't recall being scared. Looking back, I'm not sure why I wasn't. It was different from my work as a police officer. While I had arrested people before, a police officer's role is primarily to act as a deterrent. Just by being visible, a police officer prevents crime. People slow their cars down when they see a police car. They also think twice about doing something illegal when police are around.

Amazingly no injuries or deaths resulted from any of our operations during my two years with the warrant squad. This was in part because of the way we organized each operation, the many precautions we took, and our care to do everything by the numbers. We were prepared, and everyone—including the people we went after—knew it.

No matter how prepared you try to be, there are always incidents that you cannot control. While I was working in the squad's fugitive unit, five men escaped from the federal prison in Lorton, Virginia. The local corrections officers found four of them on the same day. Since federal escapees are the U.S. Marshals' responsibility, I was assigned the job of finding the missing man.

After weeks of trying to locate him using our standard investigative techniques, we learned that he had a girlfriend who worked for the Department of the Navy. At first, she wasn't very cooperative, so I told her that it would be better to have us find him than the local police. Typically, a police department takes no chances with an escaped convict and is more prone to shoot first and ask questions later. That information, combined with telling her that harboring an escaped felon could result in her losing her job, convinced her to tell me when he was coming to see her.

On Friday night my partner and I were staked out on Georgia Avenue waiting for the escapee to arrive at his girlfriend's house in his white Cadillac. When the car pulled up, I told my partner, "I'll get the driver because he's the guy we're after. You take the guy in the passenger's seat."

As we approached the car, I identified myself as a federal officer and told our man that he was under arrest. I didn't know that my partner was behind me; he was supposed to be on the other side of the car covering the passenger. As I reached out to grab the escaped prisoner, the man in the passenger's seat pulled out a .357 magnum, aimed right at my face, and pulled the trigger. The gun misfired three times, producing nothing but a loud snap. It just wasn't my time to go.

We wounded the passenger in the arm, took him to the hospital, and put the prisoner back in jail. The next morning I took the passenger's gun to the range. In order to charge him with assaulting a federal officer, we had to determine that the gun worked. We fired it seven or eight times; it worked every time. That's when the realization of what had happened hit me. Because things had occurred so quickly the night before, I had no time to be frightened. When the gun went off in the range, I fainted. They gave me some time off to recover because I was emotionally drained.

Executing warrants today is far more dangerous for a number of reasons. It's easier for a criminal to obtain a gun and to find powerful automatic weapons. If they have the money, there are people willing to sell them whatever they want. But it's also more dangerous today because people seem to have little respect for law enforcement. Perhaps this attitude is the result of being mistreated by police officers. There seem to be many more street gangs with members who don't mind dying and don't mind hurting you. It's a different ballgame than it was years ago. Despite these problems, the Marshals Service has incorporated many new approaches into its operations, including its own SWAT force, known as the Special Operations Group. When needed, these specially trained marshals can be called in to support a warrant squad.

Regardless of how many times I worked with the warrant squad, I always had it in my head that I wanted to be more like Joe Crown. Joe was always by himself when he went after criminals. While I knew that approach didn't make sense, I was young and foolish and wanted to try it.

Driving into the job one morning, I was headed down South Capitol Street and saw a man cutting wood with an ax. Recognizing him from a warrant, I stopped my car, got out, and approached him. In the process, I kept my distance in case he decided to take a swing at me with the ax.

After confirming his name, I produced my marshal's badge. "I'm Deputy Marshal Louie McKinney," I told him. "You're under arrest." He quietly put down the ax, and I handcuffed him and led him toward my car. Although I was initially a bit frightened at approaching him, I was optimistic about the reception I would receive for apprehending him.

When my boss saw me, he was not at all happy that I had single-handedly apprehended a wanted man. He chewed me out for a long time because I did it on my own. "Don't ever do that," he told me. "Don't you ever arrest anybody by yourself! You call for help. That's why other people are here. You'll get yourself killed or hurt."

After that I didn't try to be like Joe Crown again. I was happy to be part of the team and proud to be wearing a deputy's badge, the same badge that had been known as America's Star throughout the long history of the Marshals Service.

4
Before Con Air
Transporting Criminals in My Car

I was behind the wheel, headed toward Springfield, Missouri, in the spring of 1968. Carlton Elliot, another deputy U.S. marshal from the Washington, D.C., office, was in the passenger seat beside me.

In the backseat was a particularly troublesome prisoner. We were transporting him from the jail in Washington, D.C., to a federal prison in Springfield. At the time, Springfield was the only federal prison with medical facilities capable of providing care beyond what was available in most prison infirmaries. While I don't remember what this prisoner was sentenced for, I do recall that he kept making vague threats. He swore that he would escape before we arrived in Springfield. I was glad that transporting prisoners always involved two deputies: one drove while the other watched the prisoner. This man was certainly someone that we wanted to watch a bit more closely because of his remarks. While it might have been empty boasting, we were safer if we treated it seriously.

Marshals have always been responsible for transporting federal prisoners. If a criminal arrested in Virginia is wanted on a federal warrant in California, the marshals will get him there. Before automobiles were available, prisoners were transported on horseback through the frontier and on wagons pulled by mules. Anytime a federal prisoner has to be moved—whether it's to another prison or to a courtroom—he's transported in our custody.

We were limited to daily trips of three hundred miles or six hours. When

41

we stopped, we would take the prisoner to the local jail, where he would be fed, showered, and housed for the night. The deputies would stay at a motel, have dinner, and maybe see a movie. Early the next morning we'd return to the jail and carefully search the prisoner before putting him back in the car. We would also sign a receipt that allowed the jail to bill the government for the prisoner's overnight stay.

We were just getting back on the road after stopping for the night near Wheeling, West Virginia. In those days the Marshals Service had no departmental vehicles because it was essentially a low-budget operation. Whenever we had to transport a prisoner any distance, we used our own cars. No one minded because we were paid six cents a mile. If the trip required an overnight stay, we were given another fifteen dollars each to cover our daily living expenses. Many deputies signed on for this work simply for the extra money. We always found ways to cut corners so we could keep our expenses down. With the prisoner stashed in the jail, we'd often split the cost of one motel room with two beds.

Moving prisoners on a long trip was one of the most dangerous jobs that we were asked to do, however. Spending four or five days with criminals in very close quarters gives them the opportunity to study your habits and become familiar with how you operate.

Typically, we transported prisoners in leg irons, waist chains, and handcuffs. Once they were in the car, we removed the leg irons to make them more comfortable during the long trip. But they remained handcuffed at all times, even when they were eating or going to the bathroom. You couldn't be too careful. We avoided taking prisoners into public restaurants, typically using a drive-through at a fast-food joint or buying food to make sandwiches so we could eat in the car. The only time a prisoner left the car was to enter the local jail on an overnight stop or on a closely supervised trip to the bathroom. We made a point of always watching our prisoners very closely, even when they were eating.

When you're driving long distances, it becomes difficult to stay constantly alert. When we were transporting our prisoner to Springfield, we agreed that my partner would take a quick nap after lunch so that he could take a turn at the wheel. Even though I was driving, I regularly glanced in the rearview mirror. I noticed that this prisoner kept moving around. At times it appeared that he was trying to stand up.

Sensing that something wasn't right, I slowed the car so I could get a better look. I turned around just in time. Seeing something in his hand that looked like a straight razor, I jerked the car to the side of the road.

Carlton had already drawn his gun. He knocked the piece from the prisoner's hand and fired a shot but didn't hit him. The prisoner immediately changed his tune and began hollering, "Don't kill me! Don't kill me!" But it quickly became clear that was exactly what he had planned. The night before, the prisoner had obtained a lid from a tin can that was being used as an ashtray in the cellblock. He managed to file it as sharp as a razor and came very close to cutting my throat.

Our mistake was not searching him thoroughly after we left the jail in West Virginia. When we began searching him, the sheriff said that he'd already done it. "Don't worry about it, boss," he told me. "We took care of it. Your man's clean."

It was a lesson that I'd never forget. When we picked the prisoner up that morning, I was too quick to trust the sheriff. "If the sheriff searched the guy, that's OK with me," I thought. Not adhering to our standard procedures had nearly cost me my life. When you're transporting prisoners, as I mentioned earlier, you can never be too careful. You have to remember the details on a criminal's rap sheet at all times, and you can never let your guard down for a moment.

The dangerous job of moving prisoners was also complicated by the many add-on trips we would get. Typically, we'd start out with the relatively simple task of taking a prisoner from one location to another. When we arrived at the prison, headquarters might ask us to take a new person to yet another prison.

On one of my first trips, we took a prisoner from Washington, D.C., to Danbury, Connecticut. When we arrived at the federal prison in Connecticut, we were given a prisoner to transport to Leavenworth, Kansas. From there, we had to take another prisoner to Lompoc Federal Prison in southern California, more than 1,700 miles away. We were on the road for more than two weeks.

Since the Marshals Service was paying our mileage, we were not supposed to ride around without a prisoner. That would've been like having a commercial airliner flying with empty seats. It's not something the main office likes to see. As long as we were on the road, we had prisoners to transport between federal prisons. Over the years I also transported a number of high-profile prisoners. After former Charles Manson follower Lynette "Squeaky" Fromme was sentenced for the attempted assassination of President Gerald Ford in 1975, I took her to the federal prison in Alderson, West Virginia.

The training we received for this dangerous work prepared us for a variety of situations. We were taught how to read prisoners while transporting them, learning techniques that helped us to detect clues and spot problems before they happened. After surviving many days in close quarters with prisoners, I began to be able to predict their actions.

While the prisoners could be volatile, sometimes they provided unexpected comic relief. One day I was discussing our need for more cash for our trip with my partner. Hearing the discussion, the prisoner in the backseat—a polite guy named J. D. Hannon—leaned forward and offered a solution.

"Deputy," he said to me, "you've been so nice to me and I'd like to return the favor, sir." Pointing with his handcuffed hand, he continued. "There's a bank right there. Give me your weapon, and I'll happily get you all the money you want."

Despite our training, there were always situations that we couldn't possibly predict. My wife, who had taken the required matron training, came along whenever I had to transport a female prisoner. On one particular trip, we were taking a prisoner from Washington, D.C., to a prison in Montgomery, Alabama. On our way down south, we stopped briefly in North Carolina to get gas. The attendant who waited on us spent a very long time cleaning the windows. He kept wiping and wiping and wiping. I started wondering, "My windows really aren't that dirty. What's wrong with this guy?"

When he finally finished, we paid him and left. We weren't too far down the road when we heard sirens and saw the flashing lights of approaching police cars. The North Carolina state police and the local sheriff quickly surrounded us. The instructions blared over the loudspeaker, "Pull over to the side of the road." Once I stopped the car, my wife and I were told to get out with our hands up.

Seeing the police with their hands on their guns, I was afraid that one of us might get shot. I nervously asked, "What's wrong, officer?"

"I was told that you were kidnapping a white lady, that you were kidnappers," the trooper replied.

Our prisoner quickly defended us. "Hey, officer," she said. "I'm on my way to jail. I'm his prisoner, and he's a U.S. marshal."

Looking from the woman to me, the trooper asked if I had identification. When I told him where it was, he reached inside my coat pocket to get my credentials. I could see the embarrassment on his face as he handed them to the sheriff. Everyone started apologizing at once. That night we put the prisoner in the local jail and the sheriff treated us to dinner at a nearby restaurant. In the morning we were on our way again. While that incident turned out well, it demonstrates how difficult life could be for a black marshal transporting a prisoner through the South.

Because deputies had to use their own cars to transport prisoners, the service began putting requirements on the types of cars we could use. They told us that we couldn't buy economy cars; we had to use big sedans so that the service never had any complaints that we were forcing prisoners into the backseats of tiny cars. One deputy decided to fight the requirements because he was nearly fired for not having the right car. "If I'm paying for this car, you can't tell me what kind of car I have to buy," he said.

We all watched the court case closely. The judge ruled in favor of the deputy, saying that if the government wanted us to have certain cars, they would have to pay for them. That's when the Marshals Service started its fleet of vehicles. Because the mileage rates we were paid had increased, many deputies were unhappy. The fleet of new vehicles meant that we would lose the mileage expenses we were paid on these trips.

The process for transporting criminals has been radically improved since I drove around with prisoners in the backseat of my car. The marshals realized that the entire process could be made more efficient by establishing a master schedule of each district's transportation requirements. This led to the creation of a national transportation system that coordinates prisoner movements. While our work used to be limited to handling only federal prisoners, today the Marshals Service operates an efficient national transportation system that also handles the transportation of military, state, and local prisoners across the nation and around the world. This elaborate system, which is known as the Justice Prisoner and Alien Transportation System (JPATS), includes several types of aircraft and ground transportation that move many thousands of prisoners every year.

One element of our prisoner transportation system even has a rather well-known name. One day a prisoner waiting to be transported asked me how he would be getting to his destination, a federal court that was a few hundred miles away. Smiling, I looked at him and said, "You'll be traveling on Con Air." When I explained that it meant "Convict Airlines," he thought it was particularly funny and began spreading the word. The name stuck. Some years later I learned that a movie was released with the same name.

The improvements in prisoner transportation have also made this process much safer. While it used to take days to move one prisoner, it now takes only a few hours. Under the watchful eyes of a crew of deputies, we can now move many prisoners in leg irons and handcuffs in specially equipped planes.

I'm particularly thankful for the improved safety. Back in the days when we relied on our own cars to transport criminals, we all knew that this work was extremely risky. Some deputies paid the ultimate price.

When a member of a prisoner's immediate family died, a surviving family member could request that the court allow the prisoner to attend the funeral. When one prisoner's mother died in Washington, D.C., we went to Lorton, Virginia, to escort him back for the funeral. On the morning that I was supposed to take the prisoner to the funeral on Florida Avenue, I became ill. I was young and went to the office anyway. One of the other deputy marshals, a man named Norman Sheriff, could see that I wasn't myself.

"Son, you're not feeling well, I'll take the detail for you," he said. Norm always called me "son." He was one of the nicest guys I'd ever worked with. I tried to argue with him, but he eventually convinced me.

When Norm walked out of the church after the funeral, the prisoner's brother and two other men confronted him. They shot him twice in the chest, killing him, and took his prisoner. It was September 24, 1971. Today we no longer allow trips to family funerals.

Every law-enforcement officer understands the hazards that come with the job. Because the Marshals Service is comparatively smaller than other federal agencies, we lose a higher percentage of agents. Over the service's history, more than two hundred marshals have been killed in the line of duty. We all know that danger comes with the territory. When it hits close to home, it's still difficult for us to deal with.

I lived with survivor's guilt for a long time. I informed Norm's wife and family about what happened, and I felt so terrible. I kept thinking that I should have been killed, not him. He took the detail because I wasn't feeling well. He was doing me a favor and lost his life in the process. While there are resources to help deputies cope with such traumatic incidents today, there were no such programs at the time.

In May 2002 I attended a ceremony in New York that honored federal agents who were killed in the line of duty. There are many ceremonies like this that honor our fallen heroes, especially since September 11, 2001. At this particular event, Gen. Colin Powell was a guest speaker and the ceremony included pictures of the many agents who had given their lives. When they showed Norm's picture, I broke down in tears. Even though it had been many years, the sadness never left me.

After the ceremony, I saw his family and we all cried together. I told them how fortunate I was to be alive because of his sacrifice. They hugged me and told me how often he had talked about me. I'll never forget Norman Sheriff. It's because of him that I'm still alive today.

5
A Long Bus Ride
Enforcing Integration in the South

The situation seemed unreal, like a scene from an action movie. Here I was, along with a dozen other marshals, holed up in the basement of an elementary school in Columbia, South Carolina. We weren't doing undercover work, wiretapping suspects, or staking out escaped fugitives. We were hiding from the state police.

The U.S. attorney general sent us to Columbia in the early 1970s to enforce a federal law that the local and state officials refused to obey. The local opposition to our assignment escalated rapidly, and we found ourselves threatened with arrest by the state police. Unless we received reinforcements, we knew that we'd be unable to perform our duty: escorting the buses taking local black children into what was now a desegregated school system.

Having grown up in Walhalla, South Carolina, which is about 150 miles from Columbia, I was familiar with southern culture and the school system. My brothers, sisters, and I attended different schools than the white children who lived down the street. And although my father paid taxes, the school bus did not pick us up. Even when our school burned down, going to the local segregated school wasn't an option. Instead, we walked four miles into town to get a bus to a separate school in Seneca, which was another eight miles away.

When the U.S. Marshals came to my home state to enforce the busing of children to other schools, it meant the end of the "separate-but-equal" distinction that we grew up with. In some ways I wasn't surprised by the

49

townspeople's reactions. So many of us were raised with the understanding that the races just did not mix.

When I stayed in Asbury Park, New Jersey, for a time, my inexperience around people of other races caused me a great deal of anxiety. Except for my childhood pal Hoyt, I'd never been near many white people and didn't know what to expect. I found excuses whenever other teenagers invited me to the movies or other public places. Having grown up in a segregated culture, I wasn't comfortable in another environment. Witnessing the end of the separate-but-equal lifestyle in Columbia was causing many people discomfort and anger.

Growing up in a segregated society trains people to accept racial separation and stereotypes without question. When I was a police officer in Washington, D.C., I worked with an officer who came from West Virginia. Even though he never said it out loud, his tone and his actions communicated that he wasn't pleased to be paired with me. He rarely spoke to me. When he did, it was only because he had no choice; it was never more than a few words, and they always had an angry tone. After we'd worked together for some time, he shocked me by telling me how misguided he was.

"My father told me that you people were no good, that you weren't human, and that you don't even have souls," he said. "After getting to know you, I'm appalled that I ever believed that."

The deputies hiding in the school basement with me weren't the first marshals to encounter problems while enforcing an unpopular law. Marshal David Lenox, the second marshal appointed for the district of Pennsylvania, was captured during the Whiskey Rebellion in 1794. The men who captured him were among many who resorted to violence when asked to pay an unpopular tax imposed on whiskey. The capture of Lenox prompted George Washington to send the militia to free him. But enforcing integration caused more significant problems for the U.S. Marshals.

Whenever a group of marshals traveled south to enforce integration orders, the governors and the mayors usually opposed them. In most cases these officials had the backing of the local sheriff and the state police. Alabama governor George Wallace personally blocked the entry of two black college students—Vivian Malone and James Hood—who were attempting to enroll at the University of Alabama in 1963.

Throughout our history, the Marshals Service shouldered the responsibility of protecting our country's long tradition of civilian rule. Marshals have always been the last barrier standing between civil rule and a declaration of martial law. When marshals face overwhelming odds and are unable to enforce the law, the president's only remaining choice is to summon the military.

Often helped by the military, the Marshals Service enforced the court rulings that ordered the desegregation of public schools and universities in the 1960s and 1970s. From experience, I know that separate black schools were anything but equal. Years after I left school, the Supreme Court ruled that separating school children by race violated the Fourteenth Amendment and declared this practice unconstitutional. But it would take more than a court ruling for people to change.

The Marshals Service took the brunt of the nation's anger over integration. In order for one black student—James Meredith—to register for classes at the University of Mississippi in 1962, more than 120 marshals had to risk their lives. After Meredith enrolled, the marshals provided him with round-the-clock protection for an entire year. Some deputies worked undercover, posing as students so that they could provide additional security. They even escorted Meredith to his graduation ceremony.

I had the privilege of working with some of the men who faced the enraged mob on the campus of Ole Miss the night before Meredith was scheduled to register for classes. The crowd that opposed them, which grew to an estimated one thousand people, pelted the marshals with anything they could find, even bricks. They took a bulldozer from a nearby construction site and tried to use it to break through their ranks. A bottle filled with acid hit Al Butler's arm; sniper fire hurt Graham Same, causing him serious wounds. Even though they endured a night of violent upheaval and overwhelming odds, the marshals refused to back down.

Robert Kennedy, the attorney general who ordered the marshals to escort James Meredith to that Mississippi campus, sat up all night with President

Kennedy receiving reports about the riot. The attorney general called it the worst night he ever spent. The marshals received little support from the state police and were under strict orders not to fire their weapons. They were only permitted to use tear gas—which they had in very limited supply.

The attorney general praised their courage and their restraint, "If these men hadn't remained true to their orders and instructions, if they had lost their heads and started firing into the crowd, you would have had immense bloodshed, and I think it would have been a very tragic situation."[1]

Forty years later both the state of Mississippi and the university honored the marshals and the military personnel who enabled Meredith to exercise his rights by attending classes at Ole Miss. On October 1, 2002, Mississippi governor Ronnie Musgrove, U.S. Marshals Director Benigno Reyna, and many others attended a ceremony on the campus that brought together many of the retired marshals and Meredith to commemorate the historic progress that their efforts ensured.

While we waited for some time in that school basement in Columbia, we sent word of our predicament to the attorney general, who activated the National Guard to support us. Regardless of the opposition we encountered, the country's desegregation efforts would continue.

The first time that I was sent to a southern town where the schools were being integrated, I couldn't believe that I was involved in something so significant. During this assignment—which took me to Lafayette, Louisiana—I was in my twenties and, in many ways, still thought of myself as a country boy, the son of a sharecropper. I never imagined that I'd do anything like this.

I'd always thought it was amazing that white marshals went down South to protect the rights of black people. Perhaps some marshals didn't like that particular job, but they did what they had to do. When they got there, they encountered people who yelled at them and opposed them, people from their

---

1. "The U.S. Marshals and the Integration of the University of Mississippi," *United States Marshals Service: Historical Perspective*, http://www.usdoj.gov/marshals/history/miss/08.htm.

own race. They were forced to protect themselves and, often, to make arrests. All of this was done for the sake of the school children and college students they were escorting. For someone like me, who grew up where segregation was considered normal, where we couldn't use the same bathrooms or try on clothes in a store, it was hard to fully comprehend at times. I had to pinch myself to make sure that it was really happening.

When I got to Lafayette, I was assigned to work with a Louisiana state trooper. I remember that he was very polite and treated me well. But before we began escorting the buses the next day, he wanted to be sure that I understood what we were up against. About nine that evening, he drove me past a Ku Klux Klan rally. Despite the unsettling presence of the Klan, we had few real problems in Lafayette. We had deputies riding the buses and escorting the children to their new schools. While there was some protesting and plenty of name calling, there were enough of us to make anyone think twice about causing any real trouble.

Along with a group of marshals, I participated in what many people were calling "forced busing" in other cities. In addition to South Carolina and Louisiana, we helped bring an end to the separate-but-equal distinction in Montgomery, Alabama. What was surprising, however, was the opposition to integration that we faced in Boston, where we were hit with rocks and bottles.

Whenever desegregation was being enforced, the marshals remained in the area for a period of time. This enabled us to ensure that the schools actually instituted the changes, rather than complying only while we were there. Sometimes we stayed around the schools during the day as a deterrent to anyone who might cause trouble.

When we encountered problems—like we did in South Carolina—we had to rely on the National Guard for assistance. I'm still so impressed by the actions and the attitudes of the guardsmen. They were probably all local guys. Perhaps a few of them were good ole boys. But once their units were mobilized and they were given a job to do, they followed their orders. They took an oath to protect the country from all enemies—both foreign and domestic— and whether they liked it or not, they did what had to be done. They got us out of a few tight spots and my hat is off to them.

While I felt a great degree of satisfaction in doing this job, I also understood the sadness and the fear felt by the children. Many of those kids didn't want to go to another school. They were content to stay right there in their own world. Suddenly they were told that they had to attend school somewhere else, somewhere they didn't appear to be very welcome. They were afraid, I'm sure. Like me, they'd been segregated their entire lives and didn't know what to expect. While those kids might have been frightened at the time, I knew that facing their fears would create new opportunities for them and help them to grow in new and exciting ways. That's exactly what had happened to me.

After dropping out of high school, I joined the navy as a steward. I was taught how to care for an officer's quarters, to press clothes, shine shoes, and prepare meals. I loved the navy so much that I considered a naval career, but I didn't want to remain a steward. Instinctively, I knew that I was capable of much more than that.

When I approached my chief to discuss my promotion possibilities, he sent me to a seaman's course, which I passed. Even though I had that to my credit, I learned that it was going to be difficult for a steward to advance in rank. My superiors told me that my only option was to pass the third-class radio test. If I didn't pass, I would either have to remain a steward or leave the navy when my enlistment was up.

Because I had duties to perform, I couldn't go to radio school like some of my shipmates. I knew that it was a complicated test, so I studied day and night. Some of the guys helped me learn the electronics, which I knew little about.

Back then it was common to encounter folks who didn't think that black people were very smart. One chief radioman was shocked to see me studying a book on Baudot code. "Are you reading that? I didn't think people like you—" I cut him off. "What do you mean, 'People like me'?" "I didn't think black people could learn those things," he replied. "All we need is a chance," I said and went back to studying.

When the test results came out, I was the only one who passed. My superiors were shocked; they had suggested that I take the test only to appease me. No one actually expected me to pass it.

I loved being a radio operator. The work came easily to me, and I began advancing to more and more difficult assignments. Eventually I attained a top-secret clearance so that I could handle secure communications and classified information. This whole experience so motivated me that I began pursuing a high school equivalency degree while I was still in the navy.

All I needed was a chance.

Norman Rockwell painted what became a popular portrait of four deputy marshals escorting young Ruby Bridges to William Frantz Public School in New Orleans. Al Butler was working behind the scenes on the day that the marshals escorted Ruby to school in 1960. I never asked Al what he thought or what he felt when he looked at that painting—titled *The Problem We All Live With*—which was featured in *Look* magazine. But the experience of enforcing the rights of a young black girl and a black college student deeply affected him and many other deputies.

Al once told me, "It's awful that in this country we have to get court orders and provide protection to people just to make sure that they get their God-given rights."

A number of years later, when Disney made a movie about Ruby Bridges's experience, Al Butler was cast as an extra.

In *The Lawmen*, Frederick Calhoun described the effect that being involved in desegregation efforts had on the marshals involved. "Desegregating the South made them feel like they were changing the world single-handedly," he wrote. "It was a heady feeling."[2] I've heard many deputies say that these efforts changed the course of our country's history. It seemed very fitting when the Marshals Service honored Ruby Bridges in 2000 by making her an honorary U.S. marshal, a title that had been bestowed on only a handful of other people at the time.

Having deputies involved in integration and forced busing did more than

---

2.   Frederick S. Calhoun, *The Lawmen: United States Marshals and Their Deputies, 1789–1989* (New York: Penguin Books, 1991), 259.

change the country; it also changed the Marshals Service. Not too many years before, marshals had tracked down and returned runaway slaves. Now the service had brought itself—and the country—full circle. The long bus ride was over.

6
Preventing Airline Hijackings
The First Sky Marshals

At the start of another workday in the fall of 1969, I made my way down a long hallway in the Marshals Service's district office in Washington, D.C. I was heading toward what we called the "Big Room." Along with other deputies working in the district, I would receive assignments here that ranged from taking prisoners to court to serving eviction notices and finding fugitives. The assignment I got that day was not only a bit surprising, but it also temporarily moved me out of the district.

I hadn't been in the room long when an unfamiliar inspector pointed at me and said, "We need you." While I knew that inspectors often supervised special details within the Marshals Service, I still wondered what he wanted. This particular inspector, O. C. Spearman, was with a new antihijacking detail, an assignment for which our district had volunteered me. Since working on this assignment involved coming in contact with many people, including airline pilots, he wanted deputies with a neat appearance and effective communications skills. When he found out from my boss that I was a former police officer, it weighed heavily in my favor, as it demonstrated that I likely had developed the instincts needed to detect and prevent problems.

The deputies that the inspector was recruiting would fill a critical need: dealing with the many airline hijackings that were filling news reports around the world in the late 1960s and early 1970s. During this time of political unrest, it seemed that I couldn't pick up a newspaper without learning about another "air piracy" incident, which was what we called hijackings that involved ransoms or hostages. A "hijacking," by contrast, simply forced the plane to reroute to another country without making other demands.

Long before the events of September 11, armed hijackers were routinely forcing pilots to reroute planes to Cuba, Israel, or various Middle Eastern countries. The demands varied with the destinations. Some hijackers wanted the release of political prisoners; others wanted public recognition for some extremist cause. In 1970, for example, Palestinian terrorists simultaneously seized four planes headed to New York from different airports and forced them to land in the Jordanian desert. After releasing about three hundred passengers, the terrorists blew up the planes and held some remaining hostages until several Palestinian prisoners were freed.[1]

Cuba was also popular with hijackers. After the Cuban Revolution brought Fidel Castro to power in 1959, the country's relations with our government began disintegrating, especially when U.S. business interests in Cuba were seized and Castro aligned himself with the Soviet Union. It wasn't uncommon for people to hijack planes to escape his Communist regime. When the State Department banned travel to Cuba in 1962 because of the political climate, hijackings in the other direction increased in number. Some militants seeking sympathy from Castro—such as the radical group known as the Black Panthers—hijacked airliners in the United States and ordered them to Cuba as a means of free transportation.

In response to the increased hijackings, the United States declared air piracy a federal offense in 1961, making it a crime punishable by the death penalty or by a minimum of twenty years in prison. To enhance flight security, an airline or the FBI could request armed U.S. Customs agents to be onboard any flight. In later years, there were international efforts to prevent hijackings, including the 1970 Hague Convention for the Suppression of Unlawful Sei-

---

1.   Theresa L. Kraus, "New Challenges, New Duties," *The Federal Aviation Administration: A Historical Perspective, 1903–2008* (Washington, DC: U.S. Department of Transportation, 2008), 40, http://www.faa.gov/about/history/his torical_perspective/media/historical_perspective_ch4.pdf.

zure of Aircraft, which forty-nine nations joined the United States in signing. This joint declaration made it clear that hijackers would be extradited and would face severe penalties when prosecuted. In 1973 the Montreal Convention strengthened this agreement by making it unlawful to interfere with an aircraft or act violently onboard.

Despite initial U.S. efforts, a rash of air piracy incidents erupted in 1968 and hijacking became a worldwide phenomenon. In this politically charged era, one hijacking occurred about every four days between 1968 and 1972. The U.S. Department of Transportation counted a total of 364 hijacking incidents during that period.[2]

Something more had to be done; my newest assignment was part of the solution. To reinforce existing measures, a comprehensive antihijacking program was created that would place a new security force of sky marshals aboard commercial flights. To give the administration time to assemble and train this permanent force of security officers, an interim solution was needed; the Marshals Service fit the bill. At the time, we were the only federal agency with the broad range of powers needed to safeguard the airlines and their passengers. We had no limits on our jurisdiction. We could ride the planes, arrest people during a flight, and lock up hijackers anywhere.

Some people wondered why the Marshals Service got this assignment rather than the FBI. It was really a question of scope and specialization. The bureau is more of an investigative unit. It solves bank robberies and gathers the intelligence needed to build cases and charge lawbreakers. The Marshals Service, however, is primarily an enforcement organization. We had the personnel and the authority needed to enforce federal laws and, when necessary, do whatever down-and-dirty work was required. We were simply the best guys for the job.

In October 1969 our Miami office took the lead in developing what would become known as the Sky Marshal Program. An inspector named John

---

2. Judy Rumerman, "Aviation Security," U.S. Centennial of Flight Commission, http://www.centennialofflight.gov/essay/Government_Role/security/POL18.htm.

Brophy, who would eventually head the entire sky marshals operation, began working with five deputies to develop our antihijacking strategy. The operation expanded to include more than 230 deputies during the four years that the Marshals ran it. In its early days, however, the Sky Marshal Program was strictly a shoestring operation. Because we were providing an interim solution, resources were scarce. We had to resort to borrowing deputies from various districts. We weren't given much time for planning, so we had to do the best job we could with the best people we could find.

The training we received at the time was pretty basic, perhaps because the Marshals Service was already considered a fairly well-trained force. We were expected to know how to handle people and react appropriately in critical situations. We were also given detailed briefings about specific procedures and plenty of homework, with reading assignments that ensured we fully grasped these new duties.

Today the Transportation Security Administration runs this permanent security operation—which is now known as the Federal Air Marshal Program—and requires in-depth training and preparation. After a seven-week course in basic law enforcement, air marshals attend advanced courses at a special facility in New Jersey. They must master close-quarter defensive tactics and behavioral observation techniques, as well as develop precision marksmanship skills.

Today's air marshals are trained in appropriate techniques for using a firearm while flying and must meet regular qualification standards on their weapons. In the early days of this program, we were told that the last thing we should do is fire a weapon on a plane. With a high-powered handgun like a Glock or a nine-millimeter, it would be fairly easy for a bullet to penetrate the cabin wall, create a drop in air pressure, and potentially cause a crash.

Working as a sky marshal was a great assignment. Since the hijackings had an international focus, we weren't concerned with domestic flights at this time. There were six or seven of us flying internationally from Washington on airlines that were seen as potential targets. While I knew other deputies who were assigned flights to Paris, I started out riding Pan American flights to Heathrow Airport in London. Deputies I knew in New York were on similar flights. Across the country, our deputies were performing these duties from other airports. When I was flying, I always preferred to sit in the back of the plane so I had a clear view of everything that was going on. After an eight-hour flight, I'd get off the plane so that I could rest, freshen up, and get some food. About five or six hours later, I'd head back on my assigned return flight.

The excitement wore off after a couple of uneventful flights, which made these trips seem somewhat routine and boring. We weren't permitted to sleep because we were working, but it sometimes became difficult to stay awake. Drinking was out of the question, of course. We did, however, get to eat whatever food the airline served. While some of it wasn't half bad, we were also served meals that were nearly inedible.

Because we were supposed to blend in with the other passengers, we wore regular clothing and didn't identify ourselves to anyone. The only people who knew that we were marshals were the captain, the copilot, and the head flight attendant, who was called a steward or stewardess back then.

Today's airlines have reinforced, bulletproof doors on the cockpits. In those days many planes didn't even have doors. Sometimes only a curtain separated the pilot from the passengers. This relatively easy access to the cockpit made it important for us to recognize any suspicious activity quickly. Like many other former police officers, I always seemed to know when someone's behavior was questionable or when someone might be planning to do something wrong—whether I was on a plane or somewhere else. From conversations with other law-enforcement officers, I know that most of us have a highly developed sense for those things.

The only problems that I ever encountered didn't come from hijackers, however. They came from people who'd had a little too much to drink. I regularly encountered guys who became rowdy, who were raising hell and partying. Sometimes they'd try to get fresh with the flight attendants. There were also rare occasions when a woman who'd been drinking would cause a problem. When it became difficult for the crew to control someone, I would step in. I would discreetly identify myself and advise the individual—who was typically a man—that if he didn't quiet down, he would be arrested for being drunk and disorderly. When necessary, we could call ahead to ground control and have uniformed officers meet the plane when it touched down. These troublemakers would quickly be transported to jail, which made the important point that the airlines did not tolerate any type of disorderly behavior.

After a few months of these trips, our strategy for the sky marshal operation grew more efficient. Rather than trying to deal with hijackings once a plane was airborne, we realized that we needed to thwart hijackers before they boarded the aircraft. This would avoid the complicated problems of taking down perpetrators while a plane was flying. Instead of just riding the planes, we put marshals at the check-in counters and gates at thirty-three major U.S. airports. We checked the passengers using new screening equipment, monitored their behavior, and even went through their bags.

After sitting on many boring flights and dealing with drunken passengers, I took to working on the ground and found these duties more enjoyable. When I was on a plane, I knew that I was on duty for the entire flight, which made it nearly impossible to relax. On the ground, the shifts were more flexible and allowed me to take breaks whenever I needed. I also found that people were friendlier before they boarded a plane, which provided me with many enjoyable moments with some interesting people. Since everyone had to pass through our security checks, I even encountered a few celebrities. I recall having an interesting conversation with the actor Efrem Zimbalist Jr., who had starred in the TV shows *77 Sunset Strip* and *The F.B.I.*

I also met one of my personal heroes. Always a history buff, I'd read about Daniel "Chappie" James, who was a four-star general in charge of the North American Aerospace Defense Command (NORAD) at Peterson Air Force Base in Colorado. As a fighter pilot, Chappie had flown 101 combat missions during the Korean War and had been shot down twice in Vietnam, where he'd flown more than seventy-five missions. For an African-American man, becoming an officer was quite an accomplishment; becoming a four-star general was unheard of. This, together with Chappie's childhood in the segregated South, made him an inspiring role model for me. I knew that if he made something of himself, I could too.

While working at National Airport in Washington, D.C., I met and spoke with Chappie a few times as he waited for flights and was always inspired by both his accomplishments and his attitude. Because I knew that our childhood years were similar, meeting him while I was a young man greatly affected me. He had endured some tough times, worked very hard to get where he was, and was a bit further down the road of life. I looked up to him.

During one discussion, he said something that I've never forgotten. He told me, "I like to think that I got where I am because I'm damn good—not because I'm black." Chappie wanted everyone to know that his achievements came from a combination of hard work and talent. He didn't want a position or anything else handed to him because of a quota for hiring minorities. He wanted only what he deserved. Like me, he wanted to be treated as an equal by his peers.

To help prevent skyjackings, we began using metal detectors, known as magnetometers, to screen passengers for weapons before they boarded a plane. Eastern Airlines began using these devices in the fall of 1969; four other airlines adopted them before the end of 1970.[3]

The sky marshals became the first to check carry-on bags for suspicious items. We did this beginning in 1973, in response to a mandatory Federal Aviation Administration (FAA) requirement to inspect all carry-ons and scan passengers with metal detectors. Prior to this, we had conducted random checks at our discretion. Now, every passenger would be subject to the same strict procedures.

We were also provided with an FAA profile that was designed to help us spot and screen out potential hijackers. The profile we used had been developed by analyzing the identities and habits of previous skyjackers, providing us with certain characteristics that might tip us off. We looked for anyone buying a one-way ticket, paying in cash, and not checking any bags. We looked for people using identification that didn't appear trustworthy, as well as for anyone acting suspiciously. If someone fit the profile, we'd also do a very thorough pat-down search.

---

3. Kraus, "New Challenges, New Duties," 39.

Sometimes people reacted badly to search requests. We'd hear complaints that we weren't respecting a person's right to privacy; some of these refusals bordered on outright hostility. Most people agreed to let us do our job, but occasionally we encountered someone who stubbornly declined. One man, not wanting to open his bag, shouted angrily at me. When he began acting like he might get physical, I signaled for uniformed officers. With them standing behind me, I firmly and politely told him, "Sir, if you don't let us open your luggage, you are not getting on this plane."

Even after he opened his luggage, he continued complaining loudly. I tried again to explain to him the reason for the search. "We're doing this for your safety, sir, to make sure nothing happens to you or to anyone else on this plane," I said. "We are required to check anybody that fits this particular profile."

"Profile," he shouted. "You're just doing this because I'm black!"

Even though I was surprised that he'd say this to another black man, I continued explaining, hoping to reach him. I don't know that it made any difference to him, but I tried.

It was always a bit puzzling when people took these searches personally; it seemed that they had forgotten about the skyjackings that were occurring so regularly. They seemed to lose sight of the importance of ensuring their safety, the safety of the flight crew, as well as the safety of the other passengers. I searched a minister who mounted a protest and threatened us with a lawsuit, although nothing ever came of it. Reactions like these made the job very difficult at times. Today we might be accused of racial profiling; back then many of the minorities we searched accused us of discrimination. Maybe the airlines needed to do a better job of educating the public because no one seemed to understand that we were trying to prevent hijackings on the ground, before they happened in the air. Perhaps handing out pamphlets once passengers received their airline tickets might have helped to explain the new procedures and avoid the problems.

Despite the somewhat negative public reaction, the program did seem to produce results. While I wasn't personally involved in any of these specific situations, our records show that the Marshals Service prevented at least twenty-seven hijackings.[4] There's no way of knowing how many more potential hijackings were averted just because of our presence at airports and aboard planes. We heard stories from deputies about people they had observed headed toward a gate who turned around when they saw that bags were being checked. From the reactions they witnessed, the deputies knew that these folks were avoiding the security checkpoints. Chances are they had something to hide.

In some instances, the screenings enabled us to arrest drug smugglers. We heard about women who attempted to smuggle marijuana or cocaine onto planes by hiding the drugs in their underwear. The marshals in the New York airport searched two passengers who set off the metal detectors and then failed to produce valid IDs. The resulting searches uncovered illegal drugs, which had been wrapped in aluminum foil. Many drug smugglers used aluminum foil, thinking it made detection more difficult.

John Brophy stopped a man who was acting suspiciously in an airport. The man rushed up to a ticket counter immediately before the plane was boarding and attempted to reserve a seat under one name, even though his identification and his ticket showed a completely different name. Instinctively suspecting that the passenger's last-minute actions might be a ploy to help him avoid a security check, Brophy followed up. A search showed that the passenger was carrying a number of IDs, all with different names, as well as packets of heroin wrapped in foil.

During the four-year period that the Marshals Service ran the Sky Marshal Program, our deputies made more than 3,400 arrests. Slightly more than 10 percent of these arrests involved passengers carrying concealed firearms or other weapons.

It was amazing to see what weapons people carried. It must not have occurred to them that bringing a knife or a gun onboard a plane would create a problem. Maybe they were in the habit of carrying weapons every day, since some of them seemed genuinely surprised or ignorant about why we stopped

---

4.   "The Marshals Service Pioneered the Air Marshal Program," *Marshals Monitor*, January 2002.

them. It wasn't until we brought in the local police to take them into custody that these people grasped the reality of their situations.

I arrested quite a few people who set off the metal detectors because they were carrying army knives. Another popular item was the Smith and Wesson snub-nosed .38, since its compact size made it easy to conceal. I never saw any automatic weapons, but I do remember being shocked after encountering one passenger who attempted to smuggle a rifle on a plane in a carrying case that might be used for a musical instrument. Maybe he was hoping that we wouldn't notice. But the carrying case he used was unusual enough that I decided to check it out.

While we didn't see any handmade weapons on passengers coming through the Washington, D.C., airport, I knew that deputies in the more heavily trafficked New York airports confiscated a variety of these items. The marshals in New York discovered people who were carrying fountain pens and cigarette lighters that fired bullets. They also detected a cane that hid a razor-sharp blade inside it.

While hijackings occurred during the years we managed the Sky Marshal Program, none of them originated in the airports or on the airlines that we protected. One famous and still-unsolved hijacking involved a man who used the alias of Dan Cooper. He later became known as D. B. Cooper.

On November 24, 1971, D. B. Cooper was a passenger on Northwest Orient flight 305 traveling from Portland, Oregon, to Seattle, Washington. Claiming that he had dynamite in his briefcase, he gave a note to a stewardess threatening to blow up the plane unless the airline gave him $200,000 in unmarked $20 bills. When his demands were radioed ahead, the airline worked closely with the FBI.

When the plane landed in Seattle, Cooper was given the money, along with the four parachutes that he requested. After releasing the other passengers, he demanded that the pilot take off again and put the plane on a course to Mexico City. As they were flying above the Portland area, Cooper opened the plane's rear air stairs and parachuted into the night with twenty-one pounds of twenty-dollar bills strapped to his body.

Despite an intensive investigation conducted by the FBI, Cooper has never been seen or heard from again. Because he was considered a fugitive, the Marshals Service assisted with the search and pursued a number of leads, none of which were viable. Since this case involved both a hijacking and extortion, our involvement was limited, as the case was within the FBI's jurisdiction.

Some investigators believed that Cooper had probably died. They believed no one could have survived a nighttime jump that would have been even more dangerous because it was both windy and raining. They thought that he probably "splattered" somewhere. They also doubted that he knew where the plane was when he bailed out, and survival in unfamiliar terrain might have been difficult. In addition, he was inadvertently given a reserve parachute that was designed for training and had been sewn shut.

About twenty years later, a man named Duane Weber made a deathbed confession to his wife that he was Dan Cooper. She communicated with the FBI about her late husband, providing information about things that he'd said in his sleep and describing a trip they'd taken to the Seattle area. The FBI had been able to secure Cooper's DNA from a necktie that he had discarded on the plane. The results of this test disproved Weber's claim. For a while, bureau agents thought they had found part of Cooper's parachute, but the material of the recovered chute was different from those supplied to the hijacker. The only other item that's been recovered was a stack of nearly three hundred twenty-dollar bills found near the Columbia River in 1980 by an eight-year-old boy during a family picnic.

People still continue to wonder about D. B. Cooper. Musicians in the Seattle area have written songs about him and he's been mentioned in some TV shows. In my opinion, the man known as D. B. Cooper is probably living under another name in Mexico, in South America, or maybe somewhere overseas. I don't think he died after the jump because we conducted a very thorough search of the area and certainly would have found his remains. Since there's no proof that he's deceased, we have to assume that he's still alive. Maybe he's sitting on a beach somewhere, enjoying life.

Even though it's been more than thirty years since this hijacking, the search for D. B. Cooper hasn't been abandoned. Hoping to get new leads on this unsolved case, the FBI recently reinvigorated its search for him, encouraging people to learn more about the case and to provide any information they might have about the hijacker.

If the Sky Marshal Program had been more widespread, I doubt that we'd be hunting for D. B. Cooper at all. Unfortunately the focus of our program was on international travel, rather than on domestic flights. The Portland airport did not conduct passenger screenings at the time. However, Cooper fit the sky marshals' hijacker profile: he purchased a one-way ticket and paid cash for it. The marshals would not have let him on the plane.

The Marshals Service transferred the administration of the Sky Marshal Program to the FAA at the close of 1973. While we had implemented and run a successful operation, without a large increase in personnel, we couldn't continue running it on a daily basis. The security programs we instituted needed to be available at every airport with a full-time force dedicated to the job. With our responsibilities for executing warrants, providing court security, and apprehending fugitives, the sky marshals operation was spreading us too thin. The program needed its own dedicated security force.

The FAA found a great man to take over the operation and administration of the Sky Marshal Program. Gen. Benjamin Davis Jr. was a West Point graduate and had been the commander of the Tuskegee Airmen during World War II. When he retired from the U.S. Air Force, he ran the program for the FAA and was later named the assistant secretary of transportation. His father, Brig. Gen. Benjamin Davis Sr., had been the first African-American general in the U.S. Army and the first four-star black general in military history.

The two years that I spent working as a sky marshal proved to be a valuable experience, as I periodically encountered other hijacking incidents later in my career. When I was the marshal running our operations in the U.S. Virgin Islands, a convicted mass murderer sentenced to serve eight life sentences was flown from St. Thomas to a federal prison in Lewisburg, Pennsylvania. I received a phone call from the deputies in New York informing me that he had somehow hijacked the commercial flight that was supposed to deliver him to Kennedy Airport. He had rerouted the plane and its passengers toward Cuba.

While I could do little about the hijacking, my previous experience helped me to understand what likely had happened during this incident. Typically, the marshals were responsible for moving prisoners to federal prisons. Since this particular prisoner was being held in a U.S. territory, the local Department of Corrections also seemed to have jurisdiction and it wanted to assume responsibility for transporting him. Because he had just gone through a high-profile trial and was considered a pretty bad guy, the corrections officers probably thought it would be better and easier for them to transport him.

The prisoner's name was Ishmael LaBeet. He had been convicted of leading a group of men who murdered eight people at a golf course, which was then called Fountain Valley, in St. Croix. Because the Virgin Islands are a territory, the crime was considered a felony and a federal offense. The media followed the lengthy trial closely, especially since some of the victims were U.S. citizens. Reporters even began referring to the defendants as the "Fountain Valley Five." While these defendants weren't the Chicago Seven, the lawyers persisted in trying to turn the trial into a civil rights platform in order to get their clients cleared. The defense attorneys used every strategy, no matter how far-fetched it might seem. They even tried to link the murders to their clients' inability to find jobs after returning from military service, suggesting they were victims of prejudice. After all of the drama, everyone associated with the proceedings was glad that the case was over and that LaBeet would be back in prison.

During the flight to Kennedy Airport on New Year's Eve, LaBeet said he wasn't feeling well and asked to go to the bathroom. When he came out, he was carrying a gun. No one is sure how the gun was stashed in the plane's bathroom for him. But, once he had it, he forced the corrections officers to lie on the ground. Then he took away the officers' guns and hijacked the American Airlines plane and all of its passengers, setting a course for Cuba.

Changing course meant that the pilot had to get permission to land from the local air traffic controllers. He was also required to tell them about the armed hijacker. Once he landed in Cuba, the local authorities promptly arrested LaBeet. Since Cuba had no extradition treaty with the United States, he was put in prison there. Eventually we heard that he escaped from the Cuban prison and was likely hiding somewhere in Africa, where he could avoid extradition. He's still considered a fugitive from justice, he's still on our list, and eventually we'll catch up with him.

Immediately after the September 11 terrorist attacks, the Marshals Service made many deputies available to ramp up airport security. While the FAA was still administering the Federal Air Marshal Program, they had fewer than fifty armed marshals at the time. Until more qualified applicants could be recruited and trained, the Marshals Service, together with the National Guard and other military units, provided additional security.

I was the acting director of the Marshals Service at the time, and my office received a call from the deputy attorney general, Larry Thompson. Because of our previous track record with the program, Thompson wanted us to give serious consideration to taking on the Air Marshal Program on a permanent basis. Unfortunately my team ended up telling the deputy attorney general's office that we didn't have the manpower to run the program. There were just too many management, operational, and training considerations for us to overcome.

The communication with the deputy attorney general happened when I was out of town, and I didn't find out about it until I returned to the office. When I learned what had happened, I tried to contact Thompson's office to reverse the decision. When I finally got through, I learned that the wheels had already been put in motion and that it was too late for our participation to be reconsidered. That train had already left the station. The deputy attorney general told me that, given the important national security considerations, we shouldn't have focused so much on what we were lacking. "Louie, that was a bad move," he said. "The Marshals Service had a great history with this program. If you had taken this program, you could have gotten whatever budget you wanted and all the people you needed."

I was very disappointed and angry that we'd dropped the ball. In some ways, I felt that we'd let the country down. I knew that the Marshals Service could have done an effective job in enhancing airport and flight security procedures by capitalizing on our history with the program.

While today's airport processes are providing a fair amount of security, they can always be improved upon. Security personnel need additional staffing and a higher degree of training. Many guards I've encountered don't appear to be attentive to the many subtleties that indicate potential problems. Both the airlines and the airports ought to provide good management, as well as effective security. Everyone—the airlines, the flight crews, and their passengers—deserve absolute security when they travel. We all deserve the very best staffing that we can provide, as well as highly trained and alert security personnel who can deal with any threat.

The Marshals Service set a very high standard for airport security. I'm extremely proud to have been associated with the work that we did.

7
Shadow Stalkers
The Creation of the Special Operations Group

I was distracted and I knew it. My attention kept wandering from the night maneuvers that we were learning to execute. As I lay on the ground in the darkness, in a small Texas town near the Mexican border, my mind was preoccupied with a more compelling concern.

As one of the first recruits for the Marshals Service's newly formed SWAT team—known as the Special Operations Group (SOG)—I was enduring a hellish, Marine-style training camp in the early 1970s with many other specially selected deputies. We were being put through weeks of arduous physical training with little sleep, all of it designed to produce an elite tactical unit capable of responding rapidly to national emergencies, dealing with high-risk situations, quelling riots, and providing tactical support for dangerous or sensitive operations. Serving as the Marshals' tactical squad required that we be fully prepared for a variety of situations, from apprehending armed fugitives to serving warrants in cases considered too risky even for the warrant squad.

When SOG was established in 1971, it was the first tactical team formed by the federal government. SOG existed before the FBI created its Hostage Rescue Team in 1982 and before Delta Force and Seal Team Six, the military's counterterrorist tactical units, which were created in 1977 and 1980, respectively. The U.S. Marshals' elite unit would later prove itself during a long siege at Wounded Knee and at other high-risk incidents.

To reduce the element of risk, many of our operations were carried out under cover of darkness, either late at night or very early in the morning. Initially, we wore various military-style jumpsuits. Once we adopted our trademark black "ninja" uniforms, we were undetectable in the dark. Before long, the uniform and our frequent nighttime maneuvers earned us the nickname the "Shadow Stalkers." I'm not sure exactly when this name was first associated with SOG. Maybe some creative fugitives invented it after we surprised them, jumping out of the shadows to apprehend them. Wherever the name came from, it stuck.

When the Marshals' leadership suggested creating this specially trained group, the White House and the attorney general's office supported the idea. In the early 1970s there were many protests against U.S. involvement in the Vietnam War, as well as frequent antigovernment demonstrations, which often turned into riots. Calling out the military is always the government's last resort. Whenever possible, officials want to avoid having the National Guard or the military battling civilians during civil disturbances. Since the Marshals Service was the federal government's law-enforcement arm—and we'd already proved our effectiveness by enforcing integration in the South—the powers-that-be decided that we should receive whatever additional training and equipment we needed to respond to the increasing number of civil disturbances. Wayne Colburn, who was the director of the Marshals Service at the time, immediately started planning and forming this group.

Colburn was well advised about the development of the Marshals' special operations team. He pulled together an advisory group of retired military officers who knew what it took to develop a capable force that was prepared to handle a variety of hostile situations. Since the Marshals Service needed an elite team, the initial SOG training was modeled after the army's stringent requirements for their special operations units, such as the Army Rangers and Special Forces. After assembling a team of tough former military instructors to provide the training, Colburn's office sent out a teletype with orders to begin recruiting deputies for this new unit.

The deputies initially selected for SOG came from districts across the country. While I was one of several candidates selected from the Washington, D.C., office, at the time I couldn't tell you why they picked me. I thought that it likely had something to do with my background as a police officer, since my previous training and police work gave me experience in dealing with many situations. In addition, at thirty years old I was strong, physically fit, and fearless. While those qualities certainly helped, the selection criteria went far beyond physical strength and police experience. Certainly, SOG team members need the physical stamina to endure lengthy deployments in harsh environments. But it was also critical for us to possess strong mental and emotional traits. Our chiefs and inspectors put us through rigorous background checks. They examined our performance to ensure that the deputies they selected had distinguished themselves, weren't complainers, and demonstrated the important quality of mental toughness. We had to be the service's very best in every way.

Of the approximately 125 candidates who arrived for initial training in Brownsville, Texas, only twenty-six of us graduated. Every day offered new opportunities to wash out. In addition to dealing with drill sergeants screaming in our faces, we endured constant physical exertion. For twelve hours a day over nearly four weeks, we learned to qualify with various weapons, jump from helicopters, and rappel from buildings. There were daily five-mile runs. We were schooled in hand-to-hand combat, pushed through obstacle courses, and trained in tactical operations. Since we also had to be proficient in night maneuvers, we sometimes didn't get much sleep. It was very different from the basic training that I received in the navy. While that experience had some physical aspects and a lot of marching, it also included many classroom activities. There were far fewer classroom sessions for SOG candidates. Because the SOG training was modeled after U.S. Army special operations training, it was nearly all physical.

As I lay on the ground during this particular night-training exercise, I was using every sense and skill at my disposal to intently search the darkness for one particular nemesis. I wasn't trying to detect another deputy or an instructor posing as an enemy. The foe that was on my mind was even more troublesome.

Before I'd arrived in Brownsville for SOG training, I'd heard about obstacles that I would face. I knew about the intense heat. Combined with the humidity, it could make completing drills and exercises particularly tough. You had to drink plenty of water to stay hydrated. But there were ways of dealing with the heat; my other concern didn't seem to have an easy solution. I don't recall whether I'd heard about the snakes in this part of the country from other deputies in Washington, D.C., or whether someone told us about them during the training. That didn't matter. Lying on a covering of hay in the dark, I couldn't get the snakes out of my head. All I could think about was what someone had told me: that there were rattlesnakes in Texas as big as a man's arm. I didn't want to encounter one that night.

My fear of snakes probably began in childhood, perhaps even earlier than I can remember. This fear has dogged me throughout my life. When my son was a boy, I often took him fishing in the river near our home in Annapolis. On one particular weekend, we were all set for another enjoyable day—until I saw something moving in the water.

"Get in the car, son," I told him authoritatively, while trying to contain my emotions.

Surprised, he looked up from his rod and reel and innocently asked, "Why, Dad?"

"Don't sass me now. Just get in the car," I replied sternly.

When we got home, he walked sadly into the house and was greeted by my wife. Surprised that we had arrived home so early, Judy asked him what happened.

"Oh, Dad thought he saw a snake," my son replied. "It was probably just a stick."

I clearly had not masked my fear.

Maybe my son was right, but I wasn't willing to stick around and find out. I had no fears about apprehending wanted fugitives, transporting convicts, or executing warrants in potentially dangerous situations, but I took no chances when it came to these particular reptiles.

The other SOG candidates detected this weakness and capitalized on it, teasing me whenever they had the opportunity. On one occasion we were drilling, all of us marching down the road. Seeing a fallen tree limb across the roadway, my friend Bill Armstrong, who was marching farther up the line, began passing the word along: "Snake! Snake in the road." When the message reached me, I lost control. I was so petrified that I jumped into another deputy's arms. Everyone had a good laugh that day at my expense.

One day it happened. We had a joint training event scheduled with the U.S. Army Rangers at Fort Bragg in North Carolina. While we wouldn't be working with the Rangers during actual operations, training with them prepared us to develop similar skills and attitudes. The majority of the exercises involved helicopter jumps, scaling walls, and other physical activities that pushed us to the limits. For me, the hardest part was an exercise that involved climbing into a pit to evade detection. Every one of these pits contained a snake. The purpose of the exercise was to force us to face our fears. In the field, we had to be able to endure anything. We didn't have the luxury of responding fearfully. An emotional reaction, such as yelling and jumping up when startled, could get us killed.

Just being in the pit with a snake wasn't enough for our instructors, though. We could not leave the pit until the snake was dead. Luckily for me, many of the exercises involved a partner. In this case, I buddied up with one SOG teammate who was a former Army Ranger. Whereas entering the pit was tough for me, he seemed to have no reservations at all. I imagine that he'd seen much worse while serving in jungle combat in Vietnam. I'd heard that the Rangers were even trained to eat snakes, something I couldn't imagine doing. Since my partner was trained to handle the roughest situations possible, he grabbed the snake and quickly killed it with his bare hands. I was relieved when that was over.

That encounter wasn't enough for me to overcome my fear of snakes, and that got me in trouble during this night-training exercise. We were hiding in the hay, supposedly to escape detection. This exercise was supposed to simulate our penetration of a building and involved men in a tower posing as sentries. If they saw us, they would shoot us with rubber bullets.

I wasn't concerned about the bullets; I was worried that there might be snakes hiding nearby in the hay. Wanting to make sure that any darn snakes in the area stayed away from me, I grabbed my baton and began banging the ground around me. Suddenly out of the darkness came a drill instructor's voice. "McKinney, stop hitting your baton on the ground! There aren't any snakes there, and now we know where you are." He knew that it was me, he knew what I was doing, and he knew why.

Periodically a psychiatrist evaluated us. It was his job to make sure that we were able to handle the tough situations that we would encounter in SOG operations. He asked us many seemingly crazy questions. He wanted to know whether I preferred men or women, how I would react if someone called me the "N" word, and what I'd do if someone spit in my face. All of these questions had a purpose: they were designed to catch us off balance and detect how we might react in a crisis. Before instructors could expect us to handle riots and other tense situations, they wanted to be sure that we were well balanced. That's why the initial training was patterned like boot camp. When the instructors were screaming in our faces, spitting at us, and calling us the worst racial slurs they could think of, they were looking down the road. They knew that we'd be facing rioters and protestors who would test our limits. The most important thing for us was to be able to maintain control in every situation. That required keeping ourselves under control. Thankfully my fear of imaginary snakes wasn't severe enough to flunk me out.

The SOG training was beyond anything that I'd ever experienced. Since many of our deployments would occur when it was dark, night maneuvers were a frequent part of our preparation. Working in the dark provided us with the element of surprise and also enhanced our safety. Before we could skillfully maneuver at night, we had to become more acclimatized, which meant that we regularly trained in the dark for five hours or more. The actual tactics we rehearsed were often the same as those we learned to execute during the daytime; we were expected to be equally proficient at night.

While I'd been part of the warrant squad and was used to conducting raids, SOG training exposed me to completely new ways of safely entering a building during the high-risk situations that we would encounter. The warrant squad typically knocked on doors and waited for someone to answer; SOG typically skipped the knock and broke down the doors. When the warrant squad anticipated resistance from an armed fugitive, SOG would take over the operation, employing entirely different techniques and equipment. During our training, we mastered the use of battering rams and learned to make entries with shields protecting our bodies. In addition to these dynamic entry techniques, we practiced tactics for surrounding buildings and were trained in breeching techniques, which involved thrusting a big jammer into a door to force it open. We learned many methods of restraining people and tactics for taking a person down. We even expanded our handcuffing skills so that we could execute this maneuver within a required time limit.

Weapons were an important part of the SOG training. Like any competent special ops unit, SOG also had a sniper team. While I wasn't trained as a sniper, we all became accurate marksmen with various automatic weapons, as well as with pistols. The targets that we had to hit were quite a ways off, sometimes twenty-five feet or more. We had to qualify on .357 magnums and .38s and demonstrate our proficiency with both hands. You couldn't qualify only with your dominant hand. Being capable with both hands was important because you might be forced to shoot over and around various obstacles, such as cars and buildings, and might be able to get only your left side out. Because I was right-handed, firing on my left was difficult at first. I spent much of my spare time practicing "dry firing," or shooting without bullets, until I felt more comfortable with the left-side positions.

While some deputies outside of SOG might use the same pistols, they didn't have access to our automatic weapons and had to be proficient with only one hand. In addition to the pistols, we had to qualify with the M-16, which I found fairly easy. Later on, we qualified with Israeli-made Uzis. Becoming proficient with automatic weapons was useful in situations that required additional firepower. I didn't have problems with Uzis either; it seemed like a point-and-shoot situation, just like the M-16s.

Our instructors also found ways to integrate psychology into our weapons training. This aspect of our preparation was called the pistol stress course. Any time that we had to use a weapon could potentially cause stress; we had to learn how to control that anxiety.

The primary technique was to focus on what we were doing and realize that when we took a shot we would be taking someone's life. Unlike other law-enforcement officers, SOG deputies are not trained to disable someone by wounding them or by firing warnings shots over their heads. Those disabling shots are used only in movies and on television. When an SOG member draws a gun and takes a shot, it's serious business. And when we fired, we didn't fire only once. We'd follow up a shot to the body or to the head with multiple shots. We wanted to make sure that when we shot a dangerous perpetrator, we took him out for good. Like every law-enforcement professional, we knew that we had to be ready to use our weapons when the circumstances called for it.

To complicate matters, innocent people appeared during the simulations in the pistol stress course. You'd see the bad guys, but you might also encounter a lady pushing a baby carriage down the same street. You had to be careful that you didn't shoot the wrong person. There were all kinds of distractions, and that's what made this training very realistic. Sometimes you couldn't be sure whether the guy in a car was a local cop coming to help you or a bad guy. You didn't want to shoot a local cop, and you didn't want to shoot your partner either. These drills provided experiences that helped you to hone your instincts, read situations, manage stress, and react appropriately.

When SOG is called into a high-risk situation, it becomes the group's jurisdiction. (This is also what happens when a police SWAT team is activated.) The specialized nature of our training and equipment make it appropriate for us to handle dangerous incidents, such as those involving hostages, riots, or armed felons. It didn't matter who else was there, when SOG showed up, we called the shots. If there were detectives or inspectors already on the scene, they had to step back and allow us to take charge. Having SOG in command ensured that we were able to do our work efficiently and without interference from those who might not fully understand our methods. Because of that, we were also prepared to take complete control of these incidents. This included developing various situation management and leadership skills, as well as being prepared to handle hostage negotiations whenever necessary.

Just passing the initial SOG training wasn't enough. Every SOG member, like members of the Reserves or the National Guard, was required to return for two weeks of annual refresher training. We'd refine our skills, train with new weapons that were being added to our arsenal, and learn new techniques.

Over the years I remember refresher training for rappelling, parachute jumps, and self-defense tactics.

We never had much free time during SOG training. Because of the intense physical aspects of what we were doing, whenever we did get some time off, most of us would sleep. On one occasion a group of us decided to use a rare night off to visit a nearby town in Mexico. Before we crossed the border into Matamoras, we left our guns and badges behind; we didn't feel it was appropriate to identify ourselves as federal marshals while visiting as tourists.

I'd never been in Mexico before. I remember people asking my SOG teammates and me for money as we walked down the street. "I don't have any money to give you," I told them. While I was a little surprised at how much panhandling there was going on, we continued looking around. At one point, a truck pulled up containing four or five Mexican soldiers. When they put us against a wall, at first we had no idea what to do. While the situation could have become an ugly confrontation, our training had given us the confidence to figure a way out. We quickly discovered that they wanted money too. Once we gave them some American dollars, they left us alone.

Eventually the SOG training moved farther from the Mexican border, shifting from Texas to Louisiana, where it is today. Initially SOG used the same training facility as the Border Patrol Academy in Los Fresno. Now SOG has its own permanent training facility in Camp Beauregard, Louisiana. This modern building provides for enhanced training opportunities in an environment that is tailored to SOG's needs.

I encountered different reactions from people within the service when they learned that I was part of SOG. Some of the folks that I worked with were happy for me when I shared the news of my involvement. Others seemed a bit jealous, wondering why I was selected while they weren't. Many of the black deputies were particularly happy that one of us achieved a spot on this important unit.

Those of us in SOG had a slightly different perspective. We often joked among ourselves about being "trained killers." Maybe it was a way of relieving the stress of training or of various missions. When someone began teasing someone else on the team, the person who was the brunt of the joke always responded, "Don't mess with me; I'm a trained killer."

Joking aside, all of us were proud to have been selected; the twenty-six of us who made it through the training and onto the team were particularly elated. Being in SOG made me feel like I was a very special part of the Marshals Service. The distinction that came with being selected for such an elite, high-profile team meant much to me. Here I was, a country boy from the South, who grew up on a farm. I never dreamed that I'd end up where I was. I felt appreciated and privileged to serve in this way.

Many aspects of our training have stayed with me. Since my childhood, I've always appreciated any type of hard, physical effort, so I enjoyed tackling the obstacle courses and the other challenging physical activities that were so much a part of our SOG preparation. Throughout my career, I've continued running and always endeavored to stay in good physical shape. I don't do the five-mile runs we regularly did during SOG training, but because I know that physical activity can prolong my life, even in retirement I continue to run two miles on an average of three times a week.

The SOG training did more than develop us physically; it formed us into a team with a strong sense of community. Because of this team spirit, we felt particularly bad when someone didn't make it onto the team.

One particular team-related incident troubled me. I became friendly with a deputy from San Francisco during the training. Unfortunately, my friend didn't make it onto the team. I don't recall if he left on his own accord or if he was asked to leave. On the day that he left, I had been asked to help out in the supply room. All of us had shipped some personal items to Brownsville before we arrived for training; since space was at a premium, we had them stored in this room. It was my job to give my friend his weapon, his other belongings, and a ticket home so that he could return to his district. After that business was concluded, we awkwardly said good-bye. Later, we learned that he'd killed himself—using the gun that I'd returned to him. While I didn't know what else was bothering him, I imagined that his desperate act was the result of embarrassment over not qualifying for SOG. It makes no sense now, but at the time, I thought that I had contributed to this unfortunate act because I had given him his equipment on the day he left.

Staying focused during the weeks of grueling preparation was tough. Some of the guys couldn't take the daily training runs, while others couldn't handle the screaming and shouting from the instructors. Reminding them that the yelling had a purpose—to ensure that we were in always in control, even when confronted by rioters—did them no good. Some of the guys quit, while others were asked to leave because they were unable to meet SOG's strict qualification requirements. The harassment that trained us to remain in control did pay off. When our SOG team was activated to contain protesters who were threatening to enter the grounds of a federal prison, the rioters called us names, screamed racial slurs, and spit at us. I was thankful for this aspect of our preparation. During the two or three days that we were there, none of the SOG members reacted to this hostile treatment.

I was already familiar with some of the deputies who went through SOG training. I trained with Frank Vandergrift, who was also from the Washington, D.C., office; he had had the idea of assigning me to work with Ellis Duley on the warrant squad. Bud McPherson, who would go on to run the West Coast operation for the Witness Security Program, was also part of the SOG operation. Bud became a technical adviser for the 1999 film *Witness Protection*, an HBO movie about witness security that starred Tom Sizemore and Mary Elizabeth Mastrantonio. Bud and I worked together at Whitman Security after I retired as a deputy marshal in 1990.

Frank, Bud, and the other deputies who successfully made it through the SOG training all shared certain characteristics. They seemed to be more strong willed and purposeful than those who didn't make it onto the team. Once they made up their minds to endure the training and become part of SOG, it was pretty much a done deal. For all of our joking about being trained killers, some people just didn't have the mental toughness to handle that possibility. Even guys who had been in the military found it difficult to muster up the mental strength required to handle the in-your-face aspect of our preparation.

The respect we held for teamwork is probably the biggest difference in the deputies who became part of SOG. Everything we did was built on a foundation of teamwork. Even the techniques that we executed relied heavily on a spirit of cooperation. The focus was always on corporate efforts and on watching the other person's back. When we were responding to a critical situation, it was important that we looked out for each other's safety by working together. There was no room for individual grandstanding. In this environment, men who were Lone Ranger types typically weren't successful.

Once the initial team successfully completed training, we began responding to various civil disturbances. We were also activated to apprehend dangerous fugitives in high-risk situations. Whenever a fugitive had a "you'll never take me alive" attitude, SOG took charge of executing the warrant. And the team frequently played an important role in transporting and guarding high-profile prisoners, which is closely related to the U.S. Marshals' primary mission of serving the federal courts. We provided security during the trials of the Black Panthers, the Unabomber, and Timothy McVeigh, as well as the first World Trade Center bombing in 1993. We also provided protection for many federal witnesses. For example, during high-profile trials of Mafia members, we would provide additional security for informants to ensure that they didn't take a hit while they were being moved to the courthouse. Depending on the case, SOG members—wearing our trademark black ninja uniforms and carrying automatic weapons—would remain visible during a trial to act as deterrents.

When Hurricane Hugo hit the Caribbean in 1989, SOG was part of the federal force sent to restore order to the U.S. Virgin Islands. The hurricane's destructive, 140-mile-per-hour winds destroyed the island's electrical, fuel, and communications infrastructure, as well as severely limiting food and fresh water supplies. Nearly 90 percent of the buildings on the island were destroyed. The widespread looting that erupted was more than the local police could handle. SOG joined U.S. military forces in a joint task force that helped to suppress violence on St. Croix and apprehend the hundreds of prisoners who escaped from the local prison.

While SOG was an important addition to the Marshals Service, our entire operation was strictly part-time. After the training, each of us returned to our districts and continued working our regular assignments. The Marshals' first priority was still serving the federal courts and hunting down fugitives. Those of us who were SOG members fulfilled our regular duties and remained prepared for SOG activation twenty-four/seven.

Being on call for SOG was difficult at times. It was like being a doctor and never knowing what to expect when the phone rang. Many times I got a call at home at midnight and had to be ready to go first thing in the morning. Most of us kept our SOG equipment in a bag in the trunk of our car at all times. Whenever we traveled, the bag came with us. Being part of SOG also caused additional family concerns. It was bad enough that we put ourselves in harm's way by being marshals. Some wives and families couldn't understand why we had to join a special ops team and cause them further concern. It wasn't unusual to hear about a colleague whose marriage was breaking up.

SOG members faced other issues within their districts. If a deputy was on a special assignment and got a call that SOG was activated, he had to go. This often created manpower shortages. The higher-ups within some districts felt that SOG membership conflicted with a marshal's primary duties of serving the local federal courts and judges, or limited his or her ability to apprehend fugitives. It wasn't unusual for a deputy's local superiors to say, "We need you here." But the service's leadership made it clear that SOG took precedence over everything. When the team was activated, SOG members had to be released from their districts' command, much like in the National Guard and Reserves.

While it wasn't a widespread problem, some SOG members experienced resentment or jealousy from the service's "plain old deputies," who were referred to as "PODs" by everyone, including the deputies themselves. Some PODs seemed to resent what they perceived as preferential treatment of SOG members in their district. "You SOG guys think you're special," they'd say. While I didn't experience this problem in the Washington, D.C., district, or when I moved to a headquarters position, I knew that a few others on the team did.

While some districts don't like having a deputy with SOG status when they are shorthanded, having a special operations team has been very beneficial for the Marshals Service. Our role in many operations helped to expand the service's national exposure, providing us with much needed publicity and prominence.

Despite our intense training, SOG's first deployment was not without a few blunders. In 1971 we were sent to an abandoned naval air station near

St. Paul, Minnesota, so maybe it was the intense cold that threw everyone. A group of Indian activists had taken over the Twin Cities Naval Air Station, claiming that the land still belonged to the Sioux. Since one of SOG's responsibilities was to protect federal property, we went there to enforce federal law. We arrived at four or five in the morning, and the first thing that hit me when we got off the Customs bus we were transported in was how cold it was. The second thing that hit me was probably someone else's gear, as we all stumbled and fell on top of each other in our eagerness to prove ourselves.

There were certain aspects of our training that I didn't fully understand until we were deployed in actual situations; during this deployment I had one of those insights. In some ways it was similar to a scene in the *Karate Kid* movie. The boy in that movie didn't immediately understand why he was spending so much time sanding floors, washing cars, and painting fences when he was supposed to be learning to punch and kick. Eventually his teacher showed him how each job was part of his karate preparation.

While we weren't painting fences or sanding floors like the movie's main character, our instructors did devote time to having us practice getting on and off a bus. It always took us a while, and they were never happy with the results. They even timed us with stopwatches, wanting us to perform faster and faster. I wondered, "Why the hell are we practicing getting on and getting off a bus so much?" I couldn't make any sense of it.

I found out why when we arrived at this deployment. In the excitement, someone tripped as he exited the bus. Everyone who came behind him fell right on top of the other trained killers. The incident immediately impressed on me the importance of those many hours of drills that forced us to learn to move quickly in an orderly manner. There's a certain way to get on and get off without tripping when you're in a hurry. We obviously hadn't grasped that technique, but I was sure it would come up in our next refresher training.

We must have looked pretty silly. We could actually hear the Indians laughing at the pile of us lying in snow, saying things like, "Where did these idiots come from?" They must have thought we were a version of the Keystone Kops in fluorescent blue, the unfortunate color of our uniforms at the time. During the early seventies, the media was closely following the activities of these activists because of their focus on Native-American civil rights. This meant the reporters there that day had a few good laughs at our expense.

If that wasn't enough, we executed our maneuvers in expert fashion around a building—only to discover that there was no one in it. We'd surrounded the church while they were hiding in the theater. Not the best of beginnings.

There wasn't much in the way of negotiations over this sit-in. We announced our presence using a bullhorn and instructed the Indians to surrender, only to hear them say, "Come in and get us." Although some of them had weapons, they didn't shoot at us and we didn't shoot at them.

My pal Danny Dotson must have wanted to prove that we should be taken seriously after our initial foul-ups. In a demonstration of the SOG gung-ho attitude, he marched up to the theater and noticed a hole in the bottom of a door that was just large enough for someone to squeeze through. Looking at us, he said, "I'll go in there and get them out."

Before I could say, "Danny, don't do that," he crawled through the opening and was hit in the head by a baseball bat. The concussion put him completely out of action for many months, and we were all worried that he might die. Thankfully he recovered, and no one else was hurt.

After giving them a few hours, we realized that the activists were not going to cooperatively leave the building. Once we shot tear gas into the areas they were occupying, they quickly surrendered. A few of them resisted arrest, but we handled them rather easily and took everyone off to the local jail. While we were transporting them, a few of the activists recognized from my complexion and facial features that I likely had some Indian blood. My mom's mother was a full-blooded Cherokee. My father was half German and half African American, making me a mix of many racial backgrounds. Despite my mixed background, I'm still considered a black man by nearly everyone. Your family tree doesn't seem to matter; if you have an ounce of black blood, you're still considered a black man. Unfortunately, despite my Cherokee heritage, I eventually went bald, which is not something that happens to most Indians.

On this occasion, the Indians weren't interested in my black ancestors. Some of them looked at me and said, "You look like you're part Indian. Why are you fighting us? Don't you know that we're your people?" It was a line of questioning that I would face many times over the coming months and years. My answer was always the same. I'd just say, "Well, I've got a job to do, that's all."

Over the next ten days we rotated shifts so that a contingent of SOG operatives was always guarding the base that the activists had occupied. We wanted to be sure that none of them tried to go back to the buildings they'd seized. After a shift was over, we slept on the cots in the empty areas in the local jail where the Marshals Service often kept prisoners. When we thought that the naval air station was secure, our job of protecting the federal land was completed and we returned home.

During this entire operation, I remained focused, not thinking about myself, only about the job at hand. While I never worried about the potential danger, I was embarrassed at our early clumsiness and our mixed signals. Once we found our rhythm, we did everything correctly, executing the court order to remove the protestors from federal land.

Over the five years that I was a member of SOG, we were activated about ten to twelve times. We protected a federal prison in Connecticut from protestors, removed squatters who were stopping an Army Corps of Engineers project in Pennsylvania, quelled a coal miner's strike in West Virginia, and dealt with a takeover of Alcatraz Island by members of the American Indian Movement (AIM). Even considering all of these operations together, nothing came close to our deployment in Wounded Knee, South Dakota.

Wounded Knee is a tiny town near the Pine Ridge Indian Reservation. For seventy-one days, it was also the site of the longest civil uprising in the country's history—not counting the Civil War, of course. This conflict, which lasted from February 27 to May 8, 1973, was SOG's first real challenge, an opportunity to put our training to the test and demonstrate our elite team's capabilities.

The American Indian Movement, led by Russell Means and Dennis Banks, was talking about "Red Power" in the late 1960s in the same way that some African-American groups were focusing on Black Power. Inspired by what the militant Black Panthers were doing to advance African-American rights, these Native Americans formed AIM to call attention to broken treaties and Indian civil rights. To get publicity for their cause, they frequently took actions that the government found disturbing, such as occupying the abandoned naval air station in Minnesota. At the Pine Ridge reservation, the Sioux were protesting against an allegedly corrupt tribal leader and calling for an election to oust him, claiming that he was siphoning federal funds and harassing them. With the election approaching, the Sioux asked for assistance from AIM activists. The government responded by sending SOG to the reservation to ensure that there were no disturbances.

When we first got word from the attorney general's office that we were being sent to Wounded Knee, I had no idea where we were going. I remember thinking, "Where the heck is Wounded Knee?" Over time I found out more about this tiny town near the river, which had a small church but little else. Wounded Knee had its place in history long before the events that occurred in the early 1970s. In 1890 the Seventh Cavalry killed more than two hundred Indians there—including women and children. General Custer led this same unit years earlier, before his defeat at Little Big Horn.

Everyone hoped that SOG's presence would ensure that there were no disruptions while voting took place on the reservation. The strategy seemed to work and the election proceeded smoothly. While we were there, we also provided security training to the reservation's police force, offering strategies that would help it to better secure the area when we left. After being in the area for three or four days without any problems, we considered the situation to be relatively stable and made arrangements to leave. I returned to my regular assignment at our headquarters in Washington, D.C. About a week after our departure, we learned that the activists had taken over the town of Wounded Knee as part of a protest related to the voting. They actually wanted to take over the reservation's Bureau of Indian Affairs building, which housed the local police and administrative offices, but couldn't get near the reservation because of the improved local security. Instead, they seized a number of buildings in the nearby town of Wounded Knee, primarily because of the area's historical significance.

With the Indian activists in control of the town, the attorney general activated SOG, and we flew promptly to South Dakota with instructions to restore order and retake Wounded Knee. We drove from the airport to the reservation in the dead of winter, with subzero temperatures much lower than those we'd encountered on our first mission near Minneapolis. The only good news was that cold weather meant that there were no snakes. I'd rather endure the coldest temperatures than face the rattlesnakes that I've heard they have out there.

On the night that we arrived, there was a huge snowstorm that made it difficult for us to find shelter. Since we hadn't had time to make any arrangements before we arrived and there were no local motels in or near this tiny hamlet, we were forced to sleep in our cars. Because of the frigid temperatures, we kept the engines running, which meant that we eventually ran out of gas. Our individual servings of C rations and candy bars didn't last much longer. We were out of everything and were nearly freezing to death. And this was just the start of a long, cold operation that would stretch over many weeks.

Dealing with the arctic air was a constant challenge. Because of the wind chill, temperatures were routinely below zero. Often we would take a break from guard duty and head to a temporary shelter so we could get warm. But the shelters—which were holes that we dug, lined with hay, and covered with tarps—didn't provide much relief from the cold. There was no electricity, and we couldn't start a fire because the smoke would give away our position to the Indians, who frequently shot at us. I never seemed to get warm. A few of us took to carrying small bottles of Jack Daniels, sipping just enough to keep from freezing. Sometimes we'd head to our command post at the top of a hill, where one of the deputies would warm up cans of chili and beans for us. The command post was the center of our operations, where we kept supplies and communicated with headquarters. On the first day of this operation, after we set up our command post, some of us managed to grab some sleep in the vacant gym at the local school.

While there was a large contingent of both FBI agents and marshals at Wounded Knee, these teams maintained very distinct responsibilities. The FBI came in strictly as observers. Bureau agents monitored events and provided advice so that there were no civil rights violations. SOG concentrated on dealing directly with the civil disturbance, with a goal of containing the conflict and retaking the town.

At the beginning of the operation, we set up roadblocks on the four roads leading into Wounded Knee, which kept people from entering the town to bring supplies to the protestors. During my first shift, I was manning one of the roadblocks with another SOG member named Jesse. We were sent down to roadblock number one, which was just down the hill and across the bridge from the activists, a total of about a hundred yards away. It was the first time that I'd ever witnessed the war dances. Like everyone else, I'd seen them in the movies and on TV, but these were real Indians with real guns. They were beating their drums and doing what's known as the ghost dance, which reportedly unnerved army troops in the 1890s and may have contributed to the earlier massacre at Wounded Knee.

Because of my heritage, I'd been raised around Cherokees in South Carolina and knew many Seminoles from Florida. The Sioux at Wounded Knee, however, had no interest in farming. With their reputation as warriors and fighters, they were different from any of the Indian farmers I'd been around. Even for me, seeing the dancing and hearing the drumming and the war whoops up close was a bit scary. Although we would hear these sounds every morning at sunrise over the coming weeks, I never became used to them.

As we stood at the roadblock that morning and listened to the ghost dances, the sudden sound of firecrackers puzzled me. "What are those Indians doing shooting off firecrackers," I wondered. "Are they going crazy?"

The sound caught Jesse's attention too. "Get down, Louie," he yelled, knocking me to the ground. As we lay there, the car behind us was riddled with bullets from an AK-47. These Indians meant business. And, at the time, they had better equipment than we did.

Because we were concerned about raids, we dug foxholes and trenches so that we could safely and secretly observe the Indians' movements. Even with the shovels we borrowed from the local troops, digging small foxholes in that cold ground was difficult. While we lined the holes with straw for additional insulation and comfort, we knew that the Indians were also watching us. During this lengthy standoff, when we attempted to move toward or away from

our posts at the end of our twelve-hour shifts, they would begin firing. We had
to obtain armored personnel carriers from the National Guard to transport us
safely to and from our posts. Eventually, the shooting got so bad that we were
transported in helicopters.

Safety was always an important concern. Early in this mission, I drove
to Chadron, Nebraska, a small town about twenty-five miles southwest of
Pine Ridge, to get food, toiletries, and other supplies with SOG members
Jimmy Crawford, Danny Dotson, and Jack Moore. To get there, we had to
pass through an Indian village. Someone must have recognized us because
they began shooting, and we were quickly caught in an ambush. Using a
technique he'd learned in training, our driver turned over the car without
injuring anyone, which protected us while we returned fire. Someone radioed
for help, and the support from other SOG members enabled us to get out of
there alive.

While our driver's quick thinking probably saved us, our track record with
vehicles didn't sit well with the local car-rental companies. Some of them
began refusing to rent to federal agents. They became tired of having cars
returned that were shot full of holes, wrecked, and looking like they'd been
through a demolition derby.

The Indians were obviously paying attention to their operation. We learned
that a number of Vietnam veterans in AIM were organizing their resistance
and their movements. During the evening gun battles, we could often see trac-
ers on their bullets. And with the fluorescent blue uniforms we wore in the
early days of the team, we were rather obvious targets for them, especially
since these silly outfits glowed in the dark. At Wounded Knee, SOG got rid of
our "target" uniforms and exchanged them for black jumpsuits from a local
military base.

There was a lot of shooting, particularly at night, and people shot at any
sound. Most of these battles would last for hours. Thankfully the two or three
hundred yards separating our two sides kept us far enough apart for any sub-
stantial harm to occur. During the entire ten weeks, there were only three major casualties, which included the deaths of two Indians. I always thought that
this was particularly sad because one of them was a Vietnam veteran. He had

In Walhalla, prior to enlisting in the navy.

*On liberty
in Japan in
1953 with
shipmate
Harris Fries.*

*With my brother William while on leave
from the navy.*

With the team that protected Ted and Joan Kennedy.

Graduation day for the Marshals Service's first Special Operations Group.

Manning the communications center at the Pine Ridge Indian Reservation, 1972.

Riding the horse that nearly got me in trouble while at Wounded Knee.

Taking a break from guard duty at Wounded Knee, South Dakota.

Escorting the man who shot President Reagan, John Hinckley Jr.

At the Interpol conference in Cannes, France, 1983.

Ready to yell "Surprise" to a roomful of fugitives during FIST IV.

With Judy, the kids, and
John Walsh.

In costume with Bob Leschorn for the filming of a tribute to the U.S. Marshals.

With honorary U.S. marshal and astronaut Jim Lovell.

served his country and survived that war only to die on his own reservation. I was also saddened when the U.S. marshal from Nebraska, Lloyd Grimm, was shot in the back, became paralyzed, and had to leave the Marshals Service on disability. Lloyd was from Omaha, and I knew him because we'd worked together prior to this mission. I assisted with an investigation in his district, and we'd gotten along extremely well. He wrote me a great letter of recommendation because he felt that the work I did would improve his district's operations. He didn't have to do that, but he was just that type of guy.

The twenty-six-member SOG team didn't handle this operation alone. Other deputies volunteered to assist us, increasing the number of marshals to about 125. Because AIM reportedly had hundreds of people, we also received assistance from the Border Patrol, which sent people with tracking skills so that we could assess the Indians' movements. We didn't request personnel from the National Guard, but it did provide us with equipment, including the armored personnel carriers and the helicopters that we used for transportation.

While there's always been a rivalry between the Marshals Service and the FBI, we maintained a good working relationship with the agents who were at Wounded Knee. One of the younger agents didn't understand why his agency needed to be there. He told me, "Louie, you guys are supposed to deal with civil disturbances. I'm a trained criminal investigator. I don't know what I'm doing here."

"Tell you what," I replied. "If I'm going to be out here freezing and getting my behind whipped, so are you." We both had a good laugh.

I also frequently worked with one female FBI agent who seemed to have no qualms about this assignment or about having to lie in a foxhole in the freezing cold. As I got to know her, I learned that she had gotten used to rough duty from being a captain with the Marines. Years later she died suddenly, the unfortunate victim of a plane crash.

With their focus on Native-American civil rights, the AIM activists received a fair amount of publicity, as well as their own share of support. Somehow both the actor Marlon Brando and the black civil-rights activist Angela Davis managed to slip past our roadblocks to demonstrate their support for AIM. There were also many reporters writing stories about the Indians and their cause. Whenever I called family or friends, I heard about the frequent TV news reports on the situation.

Not all of the people in and around the reservation were involved in the takeover, however. I remember one woman who lived on one of the nearby ranches. She and her daughters frequently brought us hot breakfasts of eggs and sausage, which were a welcome break from the C rations that we were eating. I'm glad that she took pity on us because, being an ex-navy man, I had never become used to the canned rations. Even at sea, we always slept in beds and had our meals cooked.

A number of ranchers paid the Indians to lease land on which they raised cattle. This seemed to be one of the few industries in the area, as the land didn't seem suitable for farming. The lack of jobs out there led to poverty. There was also a fair amount of drinking among the Indians. While we were there, it wasn't unusual to hear about someone who had gotten drunk behind a house or a trailer, passed out, and then died of exposure.

While not all of the Indians around Wounded Knee were activists, some of them were uncomfortable at the sight of armed federal agents in their town and near their homes. One day I went to a small trading post to buy Indian souvenirs, jewelry, and headbands to bring home to my family. Even when we were off duty, all of us carried our M-16s because we didn't know who was hostile and who wasn't. One Indian boy who worked in the store looked at me and said, "Are you going to use that on us?" Someone else added to his remark, "We're not criminals here." My reply was always the same, "I'm just here to do my job. Unless I'm forced to, I'd never use this gun on anybody."

Another day I had a conversation with a local medicine man. As we talk-ed, he invited me to sample the buffalo stew that he was cooking. We were discussing many different things, including Indian history. Like many of the other Indians, he was curious about why we were there fighting his people. While I'd always been able to focus on what my job required, I was starting to feel torn about being there. I told him this, adding that I was feeling bad because, in addition to being a black man, I was also part Cherokee.

After I'd tasted his stew, which smelled great but didn't taste particularly good, he took me to see the historical markers that showed where the Tenth

Cavalry had camped about a hundred years earlier during the Indian Wars. This strictly African-American unit became known as a "Buffalo Soldier" regiment. These soldiers, whose hair reminded the Indians of the buffalo, had also been involved in conflicts with the local tribes.

"It happened many years ago," the medicine man told me. "You are not the first one."

As I looked up I saw the immense mountains surrounding the valley where we were standing. The realization that those hills had witnessed many years of history, together with what the medicine man had said, helped me to find my own connection with the past. I sensed that history was repeating itself and felt a kinship with those Buffalo Soldiers.

Whatever connection I sensed with the Indians and the Buffalo Soldiers nearly got me into trouble. Because I was a farm boy and used to animals, I'd managed to corral a couple of horses that had been running loose on the reservation to keep them from being hurt during the shooting. One day I decided that I'd take one of them for a ride. I'd always been a decent horseman, and I jumped on the horse while I was wearing a buckskin pullover that I'd gotten at the trading post. I completed this outfit by tying a bandana around my head and sticking a feather in it. Then I headed the horse down the road at a trot.

Somewhere I'd gotten the silly notion that it would be fun to jump the roadblock. As I neared the area, I heard someone yell, "Louie, stop! Do you want to get killed?"

Then I heard the familiar sound of guns being cocked. I had forgotten that the shifts had changed and that there were many new deputies here who didn't know me. Quickly pulling the horse to a stop, I put my hands up and identified myself. "Hold on! Hold on! I'm one of you guys," I yelled. I should have known better, but I was still young and foolish.

We had little in the way of creature comforts at this assignment. It took a month before we finally got a portable toilet at the command post. Not long after it arrived, I rushed to this new facility, which was initially perched near the top of a small hill. Once inside, I quickly removed my SOG equipment to attend to business. At the same time the helicopter used to transport us between our posts flew overhead, and its powerful rotors blew both the outhouse and its lone occupant down the hill and into the ravine. Hearing the noise and my yelling, other deputies came running to help me. When I emerged, covered in dung but otherwise unharmed, they couldn't stop laughing. From that day on, they called me by a foul nickname. "Stop it," I'd say whenever the teasing began. "Don't you know I'm a trained killer?"

After weeks of dealing with gun battles at Wounded Knee, I was cleared to briefly head home for a combination of official and personal business. To get back to Washington, I had to take a small plane from Rapid City, South Dakota, to Omaha, Nebraska, where I could get a connecting flight. As the small plane took off, one of the engines failed and we were forced to make a crash landing. No one even suspected a problem until the pilot came on the loudspeaker and calmly told us to brace ourselves. "We are going down; we are going to land. I will try to make it as smooth as possible," he said. It was a frightening situation, but it all happened very quickly. Despite my fear, I also had confidence that the pilot knew what he was doing. Thankfully, we weren't far from the ground, and he was able to put us down safely in a nearby cornfield without any injuries. It seemed like I went from one danger-ous situation to another.

As the confrontation at Wounded Knee dragged on, some of the SOG members and other marshals were frustrated that we couldn't use our tacti-cal training, automatic weapons, and armored personnel carriers to end this siege. Doing that, however, would have been contrary to the orders we'd re-ceived from the attorney general, who had decided that he wanted us only to contain the situation until arrests could be made. The White House was just beginning to deal with the Watergate crisis and didn't want more trouble. Administration officials certainly didn't want news reports about Indians be-ing injured by armed federal agents. Instead, people from the Justice Depart-ment and the Department of Indian Affairs in Washington tried to negotiate a settlement while we waited.

The negotiations went on for weeks and nothing seemed to work. To help matters along, we cut the Indians' power lines and stopped all food supplies from going into the town. This embargo seemed to help the negotiations.

Whatever settlement AIM eventually reached with the government included surrendering to arrest. We handcuffed, read rights to, and transported more than five hundred Indian activists from Wounded Knee to the district facilities in Minneapolis. While this was a bit of a trip, Minneapolis was the closest district with facilities capable of handling this number of prisoners. Some of the Indians remained defiant; others felt that they had made their point. I heard the usual questions about why was I on the other side rather than helping those who were suffering from oppression. When appropriate, I let them know that I was a peace officer first, a man sworn to uphold the law. The trials, which involved many deputies traveling to federal court in Minnesota, seemed to go on forever. Eventually I lost interest in following the news reports about them.

Wounded Knee was more than a time of testing for SOG. It was a time of personal testing. I've always been committed to whatever job I am doing, and I'd never questioned my involvement in SOG during the training. After this lengthy deployment concluded, I briefly questioned whether I still wanted to remain a part of the unit. I couldn't forget the long cold operation, the C rations, and the gun fights. In addition to being an arduous assignment, it kept me away from home for quite a while. But the pride of being associated with this elite team won me over, and I stayed.

Not long after this mission ended, I received a picture in the mail from a deputy named Wayne McMurtray, who was standing in Wounded Knee holding up a big rattlesnake. I was never so glad to see the end of an operation. I was happy that I was gone before it got warm enough for those snakes to come out of hibernation.

SOG had other confrontations with Indian activists, but none of them were the size and scope of Wounded Knee. AIM seized Alcatraz Island, which had been abandoned as a federal prison in 1963, and held it for more than a year and a half, beginning in November 1969. The organization claimed that the 1868 Treaty of Fort Laramie gave Indians rights to any surplus federal land. Hundreds of Indians traveled to Alcatraz to join the protest. The government was patient about the occupation, sending representatives to negotiate with the activists on a number of occasions.

After government negotiations didn't produce the desired results, SOG was sent in June 1971 to retake this federal property and to arrest the protestors. When we arrived, we found the island nearly deserted. At the time we thought that AIM had gotten word that we were coming and left. We later learned that the activists had found a lot of copper wire and tubing in many buildings in the prison complex. They realized that such items were worth money and began grabbing anything they thought that they could sell. Everyone seemed to think that it was more important to receive a fair share of the profits.

That wasn't the end of the story for SOG, though. Once we arrived at the island, we found that AIM had rigged booby traps everywhere. The activists had electric wires running through standing water and converted many of the prison's fire extinguishers to operate as flamethrowers by filling them with gas. They were ready for a confrontation. If their greediness hadn't moved them off the island, I'm sure there would have been casualties. After we secured Alcatraz, we worked with the local sheriff to put enough guards there to discourage the activists from returning.

Not every SOG operation involved confrontations with AIM. In 1974 we were sent to Tocks Island, which is on the Delaware River between New Jersey and Pennsylvania, to remove squatters who were preventing the Army Corp of Engineers from building a dam. The government had bought this land from the local homeowners, who then moved away. When the work on this project was delayed because of budget issues, squatters came in to take advantage of the situation by illegally staying in the vacant homes, as well as in tents, and in any other shelters they could find. They weren't protesting the controversial dam project because of environmental concerns; they moved in so they could live somewhere rent-free.

Since using the military to evict the squatters would have been inappropriate, SOG was deployed and given additional assistance from a team of deputies within the local district. As we began the operation, we discovered that many of these people were wanted fugitives and many of them were living in deplorable conditions. As we went into the different places where the squatters were living, we found guns hidden under beds and in other places. Thankfully none of them used their weapons to resist. Those who had no criminal records were escorted from the area; those who were wanted for any reason were arrested and jailed.

During this deployment I recall working with two local deputies: an attractive young blond woman and a muscular white male deputy who was easily over six feet tall. At some point, it hit me that the three of us were the spitting image of the characters from the popular 1960s television program *The Mod Squad*. We all thought that this was particularly funny, a striking case of life imitating art.

SOG was also sent to Danbury Federal Prison in Connecticut, where one member of the radical group known as the Chicago Seven was jailed. The seven leaders of this group had been charged with inciting a riot, which had begun as an antiwar protest outside the 1968 Democratic National Convention in Chicago. Worried that a similar large protest might occur at the prison, we went out in full riot gear to deter anyone from thinking about storming the federal prison to free one of their own.

Before this deployment, our team assembled in Washington, D.C., so that we could be transported to Connecticut by bus. As we approached Danbury, the bus began making unusual noises and quit on us. A team of trained killers was forced to push the broken-down bus off the road and wait for alternate transportation.

When we arrived in Danbury, we spent the night in the prison, where we had some pretty good food from the prison cafeteria. The following morning we were up before dawn and stationed in front of the building in riot gear. Over the two days we were there, the protesters continually shouted at us, calling us names, and pelted us with whatever they could get their hands on. Despite this, and the fact that we were completely outnumbered, we stood our ground. The show of force and determination paid off, and the protestors eventually backed off.

Another big operation involved a trip to Puerto Rico. Years before the island of Culebra became a popular resort, the navy used it as a target to practice shooting the big guns on their ships. The island had been used in this way for years, as the navy had always assumed that it was uninhabited. Unknown to the naval authorities, about a hundred of the island's inhabitants had not honored their agreement with the government to leave. Because of the constant bombardment, these folks occasionally ran across live shells. Yet despite these obstacles, the islanders had managed to build a small church. When naval officials discovered the presence of the islanders and their church on the island, a dispute ensued. It appeared that the islanders were trespassing on federal land. Eventually the Seabees had to tear down the church, as it was on the portion of the island used for target practice. When the navy created a restricted area by erecting a fence, the locals began protesting, claiming this property was theirs, and SOG was summoned to contain the situation.

I led the team for this mission, which included some assistance from a company of local Marines. Freshly back from Vietnam, these men were ready for a fight, which is not what SOG wanted at all. "The military doesn't fight civilians," I told them. "That's why were here, because we're trained to resolve situations like this one." Once the Marines heard this explanation, they cooperated fully and transported us to the island via helicopter. It turned out to be a successful operation: no one was injured and we accomplished the goals of the mission that we were sent to perform.

A number of years later we encountered a similar situation on Vieques, which is a nearby island. Because of the continued protests from the inhabitants of Culebra, the navy abandoned its operation there and moved to Vieques. At this point, however, I wasn't part of SOG and was only involved in a supervisory role as deputy director of the Marshals Service. The whole thing was another case of history repeating itself.

SOG also intervened in the coal miners' strike in Charleston, West Virginia, in 1977–78. When the strike stretched out over a hundred days, the government forced the United Mine Workers to return to work because of the importance of coal to the country. I knew that the miners felt they weren't paid enough and wanted safer working conditions. Until we got involved, however, I hadn't realized how dependent the country was on coal for generating power for heat and electricity.

Enforcing the government's position meant sending SOG to the mines. I had another leadership role in this operation. I took about fifteen SOG team members on a two-week mission. Our presence was meant as a deterrent, providing some assurance that the miners would adhere to the court order to return to work, as well as to keep the union activists and protesters from causing trouble.

SOG did much more than deal with civil disturbances. When the military needed additional security while it transported missiles across state lines, SOG operatives went along. We were also frequently called up to provide tactical support for other Marshals Service operations. As mentioned earlier, we also monitored federal courts during high-profile trials. Depending on the case, the SOG team might also send a couple of operatives dressed in plain clothes to monitor activities discreetly. I was a plainclothes observer during the trial of Rayful Edmond, one of the richest drug kingpins in the Washington, D.C., area. After Edmond's arrest, there were concerns that his involvement in the drug world might result in him being killed. SOG's objective was to make sure that this didn't happen.

We also provided additional security for witnesses. There was one man I remember who testified against mob enforcers who were threatening him because he wouldn't give them kickbacks from a profitable motel and restaurant he owned. Because he worked with the FBI by providing them with information, the bureau asked for our assistance in guarding him during the trial.

SOG operations have continued evolving. Since September 11, 2001, SOG members have been in Baghdad and in Afghanistan. In addition to training the local police in security measures, they assisted during the recovery of bodies and helped ensure the safety of the courts during the many ongoing trials. They often work closely with their FBI counterparts in the area.

The team has also consistently upgraded its tools. SOG has its own plane, as well as items like surveillance equipment, which we often had to beg for, borrow, and then return, when SOG was new. Other big upgrades included the two mobile command centers that provided critical service for operations like the Oklahoma City bombing. The best thing about these highly equipped mobile command centers is that they were fully funded from seized drug money.

The SOG recruiting program has helped the team grow in size and diversity, with new team members brought in every two years. Unlike in the early days, SOG now includes women. Stacy Hylton, who joined SOG in the mid-

1970s, became the first female team member. The recruiting operations are necessary because of the attrition caused by SOG's rank and age limitations. This elite unit is a specialization that's best reserved for younger deputies. In addition, once someone reaches the rank of chief deputy, he or she can no longer participate in team operations, as chiefs serve in more critical roles within their district operations and must be present to supervise their own units.

While I felt honored to become a chief deputy, it was a bittersweet moment because I knew that I would have to leave the team. Because of the intensity of our assignments, my team members and I had grown quite close, becoming our own brotherhood. "SOG now, SOG forever" is more than just an expression. Team members might leave the operation, but they're still considered part of the SOG family and they gather for regular reunions.

Throughout my career with the Marshals Service, my SOG plaque has always had a special spot on my office wall. There have been many times that I wished I could put on my SOG badge and uniform and join the team on a mission. I particularly wanted to join SOG for the operations in Baghdad.

When I became deputy director for the Marshals Service, SOG provided some much-needed support during a number of high-profile drug-related trials in San Juan. A number of us were present for these trials, which were held in a very old-fashioned courthouse. Because the judges had already been threatened and the drug dealers' property had been seized, we heightened security by activating SOG. A few hundred protestors who thought the drug dealers had been targeted by the authorities from the mainland were protesting outside the courthouse. The protests caused a number of disturbances, which led to more than a few arrests. One day, as I was driving through San Juan with the director, we noticed that a car was following us. Our SOG escort also spotted this and quickly maneuvered his vehicle between our car and the one tailing us. Then the other SOG members quickly opened the back door to let the guys pursuing us catch a glimpse of their automatic weapons. This proactive stance clearly communicated that they meant business.

As acting director of the Marshals Service, I paid close attention to anything that the team did. While the service's budgets could sometimes prove troublesome, justifying SOG expenditures was never a problem. Being in the position of activating this team, however, was always a unique experience. Whenever an executive order came from the attorney general's office, the team was deployed on a new mission. As my office issued these directives, I imagined the wheels of the SOG operation turning, as deputies were always given a set time limit in which to report for an assignment, one that varied with the type of operation. Being on that side of an SOG operation was something that I never dreamed would happen to me. The first time that I activated SOG was to deal with a civil disturbance; the last time was to respond to the events of September 11.

SOG has always filled a distinct void within the service and has also provided many benefits. Because it increased respect for the Marshals Service, it helped us to attain bureau status within the Justice Department, as well as to develop specialized skills, roles, and career paths. Within the service, SOG members are typically the top performers in whatever they do. As a director, I always favored SOG people for promotional opportunities. I never gave them special consideration if they didn't deserve it, but SOG members were consistently more seasoned and better trained. They were also more astute in reading and dealing with people and could handle any problem that was thrown at them. I was never disappointed.

Late in 2007 I was near the SOG training compound at Camp Beauregard and decided to pay an unannounced visit. Since I was in the area, I wanted to see some of the guys. I was as happy to see them as they were to see me. Many of them expressed what good care I'd taken of them during my stint as director.

I was particularly thrilled when I noticed that a picture of me, taken when I served as director, was hanging on the wall in their offices. This elite team was proud of me—one of their own—which was a distinct honor. They wisely attributed my rise within the organization to my SOG training and preparation. They're probably right about that.

8
Inventing Identities
The Witness Protection Program

As the studio audience looked on, the television cameras broadcast us into thousands of living rooms across the country. One by one, each of the three men on stage said, "My name is Louie McKinney." Only one man was the genuine item; the other two were pretending in order to fool the participants in the popular game show *To Tell the Truth*. By the end of the program, the contestants had to guess which one of us really provided new identities to Mafia informants and others whose lives were endangered because of their testimonies in court.

The Witness Protection Program was still relatively new when this episode aired in 1976. The publication of a controversial book about witness protection put our operation in the news frequently, causing our work to capture the interest of the producers of this popular game show. Eager to get someone from Witness Protection on their program, and not knowing where to begin, they called the Justice Department and were directed to us. The producers wanted someone who knew the program inside and out, had a neat appearance, and was fairly well spoken. Since the Marshals Service ran this operation, the request was referred to my boss, Jack Cameron, who at the time headed the U.S. Marshals' witness protection operation. Both Jack and the service's communications office thought that I'd be the right person for this job.

I'd been working as a witness security specialist for a number of years, after my transfer from the Washington, D.C., warrant squad. My friend Otto

Stocks had been working with this new team and recommended me for a position when the operation was still relatively new. I'd known Otto from our days as D.C. police officers. While I liked the idea of working with him again, I questioned whether leaving the warrant squad was the right decision. I was hesitant about parting with a more active assignment for what seemed like a desk job in a new operation. Like anyone else, I found it difficult to leave something known for something unknown. Still in my late twenties, I enjoyed the action that came from tracking down fugitives and executing warrants. I'd done plenty of paperwork in the navy and while working the desk as a police officer, so I knew what it was like.

As I spoke with Otto and the other deputies working in this operation, I learned that the Witness Protection Program had its start in the early 1960s when Joe Valachi testified before Congress about organized crime in return for immunity from prosecution. Valachi was the first Mafia informant, but his testimony didn't lead to the prosecution of other criminals. It did, however, provide the first detailed look at the inner workings of this secret organization. Since Valachi said breaking the Mafia's code of silence would put his life in danger, the Justice Department protected him by keeping him in solitary confinement at various facilities until his 1971 death from a heart attack. As other mobsters became informants, the witness security operation had to be handled by a separate organization so that the government's cases were free from accusations of buying testimony. Because our connection with the courts made this job a natural fit for us, the Justice Department asked the Marshals Service to take over this responsibility.

The plan to safeguard Mafia witnesses paid off. As a result of valuable testimonies from protected witnesses, the government's attorneys obtained a conviction rate of 89 percent. Every fact that I learned about this new operation fascinated me. Even though I'd been a police officer, the little I knew about the Mafia and "organized crime" came from news reports about their illegal, shadowy activities. It never occurred to me that crime was organized; I'd always thought of it as random. The notion of organized criminal activity aroused my curiosity. I knew that I'd be dealing with hired killers and criminals who fleeced people out of their money, yet I felt an odd attraction to the assignment. I became increasingly more interested in dealing directly with people like those portrayed in movies such as *The Godfather*. Because I enjoyed seeing new places, another big plus of the new assignment was the frequent travel required to escort witnesses to court and to the locations where they'd begin their new lives. As much as I liked the warrant squad, the only traveling I did there involved taking prisoners to the local district court for sentencing on Fridays, a boring chore that I certainly wouldn't miss.

I headed to the Witness Protection Program office on Twelfth Street NW for an interview with Reis Kash, the head of the Marshals Service component of witness protection. Reis worked closely with Gerald Shur, the attorney in the Justice Department's Office of Enforcement Operations who assembled the entire witness security operation in 1970. During the interview I learned that once the Justice Department determined which witnesses needed to enter the program, the Marshals Service would take over and begin the day-to-day work of creating the new identities and ensuring each witness's safety. Reis's impressive background in the army's Criminal Investigation Command (CID) qualified him to manage our piece of the program. In those early days, ours was very much a fly-by-night operation. There was only a skeleton crew in the main D.C. office providing support to the seven deputies who worked directly with witnesses in the field. The first deputy to work in the D.C. headquarters operation was Otto, who was later joined by Jimmy Calisantos and Jim Gardner. Since there was plenty to be done and just the four of us, I jumped in fairly quickly, learning the ropes of acting as a liaison between Justice, the Marshals Service, and the witnesses. Before long I was preparing the documents that the witnesses needed and became involved in creating their new identities.

Not many people realize that the same program that changes identities for witnesses had its own small identity crisis over the years. When the program was initiated, it was known within the Justice Department as WISPER, which stood for Witness Intelligence, Security, Protection, Enforcement, and Regulation. After a while, this lengthy identification was shortened to Witness Security. Those of us who worked there called it "Witsec."

Somewhere along the line, there was yet another renaming, which created the popular title everyone is familiar with: the Witness Protection Program. But it was this new name that caused problems for me during one appearance before Congress. During my testimony, I mistakenly used the outdated term "Witness Security Program." One congressman quickly interrupted me. "Mr. McKinney," he said politely, "isn't it Witness Protection? We all thought it was the Witness *Protection* Program." I assured him that he was right and apologized. I'm still not exactly sure about the date or the reason for this name change. I have to wonder whether our own preoccupation with changing identities for witnesses somehow came back to bite us.

Whether we called the program Witness Security or Witness Protection didn't matter to the television producers who were excited to have us as the focus of their game show. I don't think that anyone was more excited than I was. I couldn't believe that a country boy like me would be appearing on such a popular program. A week before the episode was filmed, I flew to New York to prepare the two men who would pretend to be me. Getting them ready to answer questions from the show's panelists was difficult at times, since there were many things about our procedures that I couldn't divulge to anyone. Somehow I managed to give them a good overview of what we did, but after a couple of days of this preparation, I grew tired of talking about it. In the end, we decided that they had to keep their answers short. While I was in New York preparing for the program, the network wined and dined the three of us, showing us around the city like we were celebrities. Even though we'd talked about witness security most of the day, everyone still asked questions during dinner. They were fascinated and wanted to know more about what I did, what Mafia witnesses were like, and how everything worked.

If those TV producers had more details about our operation, I wonder if they might have reconsidered having us on the show. When I first joined Witsec, we weren't very well organized, mostly because everything we did was brand new to us. We were always short on resources and people in those early days. I didn't have any office space, which forced me to work out of my car much of the time; I even resorted to keeping files in the trunk. Reis, who had a background in military intelligence, thought that we were living in the Marshals' frontier past. In Pete Early and Gerald Shur's book *WITSEC*, the authors write, "Not much had changed from the old Wild West days. The deputies had simply substituted automobiles for horses."[1] But the scarcity of funding and resources didn't stop us. We all knew that we were involved with important work, so we did the best we could with what we had. My new job didn't have the action of the warrant squad, but the longer that I was with the program, the more I realized how much the work suited me.

The first case I was involved with focused on Joe "the Animal" Barboza, who had been a hit man in the mob's Rhode Island operation and admitted to twenty murders. His 1967 and 1968 testimonies enabled the government to put away a number of other mobsters, including Ray Patriarca, who was said to be the head of the Mafia's Rhode Island operations. Like all witnesses, Barboza first had to be approved by the U.S. attorneys in the Justice Department before he could enter the program. Some witnesses are involved in federal cases, whereas others testify in important state cases. In every situation a U.S. attorney's stamp of approval is required. Regardless of where the case originates, the Justice Department verifies that every witness has information that's important to a government case and that his or her life is in imminent danger. Once that's determined, the Marshals Service takes responsibility for the witnesses' safety. In the process of protecting witnesses, we also have to complete a fair number of reports. We document the witnesses' behavior, describe where we transport them, list the names of each deputy assigned to every shift on the protection details, and even report whether one of our own attorneys comes to see them. This part of the operation reminded me of the old saying, "No job is finished until the paperwork is completed."

We found many ways to ensure witness security. Early on we isolated our witnesses in a separate area of federal prisons to keep them away from other inmates for their safety. In New York, for example, we had a separate floor in the federal detention center known as "the Tombs." Later we developed "safe sites" in many key areas that enabled us to house witnesses outside of prisons and transport them safely to court. We've guarded many witnesses like this,

---

1.   Pete Early and Gerald Shur, *WITSEC: Inside the Federal Witness Protection Program* (New York: Bantam Dell, 2002), 128.

providing them with protection twenty-four hours a day, seven days a week to ensure that nobody is able to harm them.

Even prisoners serving jail terms are released into the Marshals' custody once they're approved for the program. I remember one witness serving a twenty-year sentence who was signed over to us. We kept him in a safe site, where he served the rest of his sentence. At the time this was a better alternative to keeping him confined in a prison, since other prisoners could have been paid to kill him.

As soon as they're approved by the Justice Department, witnesses who need new identities are relocated with new names. Sometimes these identity changes occur before the witnesses testify so that we can move them out of what's known as the "danger zone," the area where they lived or gave their testimony. When a witness has to return to the danger zone to give testimony, we surround him or her with high security.

Not everyone is approved for the program. There have been times when a state attorney, a prosecutor, or a detective has promised this protection to a witness as bait to get information, even though the case does not meet our criteria. Once we investigate these cases, we typically turn down the requests. There are also witnesses who make up stories in order to get payback from the government. Others have good information but their lives are not in danger. Typically our investigations will determine the credibility of the witnesses' stories and their claims.

It was my job to get the real names of approved witnesses from the Justice Department and begin reviewing each case. We'd learn everything about them: whether they were married, what family members needed to be relocated with them, what cases they were involved in, and who was putting them in danger. Then, I'd assign them to our deputies in the field. For example, if a witness had to be picked up in California, I'd make the arrangements with our deputies in that area. Since witnesses were frequently involved in FBI cases, I'd also have to contact the bureau's agents in charge and communicate with them about the aspects of our operations that they needed to know. I also arranged for witnesses to get the documents they required to establish their new identities, including birth certificates, driver's licenses, and Social Security cards.

I also selected the appropriate area of the country where we would relocate a witness, working with our deputies to transport them and get them settled. We have a number of places where we send witnesses to keep them safely out of the mainstream, areas where there is no organized crime activity or little risk of them being identified. Our local deputies remain in regular contact with each witness.

Relocating witnesses is no easy task. Dealing with real estate, for example, can get quite complicated. If a witness owns property that he or she purchased with drug money, it's simply auctioned off and the proceeds go into our treasury. This money is then used to fund additional training or equipment.

Once witnesses enter the program, their personal priorities must change. Their decisions can no longer be based on how much money they'll make. Instead, their new priority becomes whether or not a decision will keep them alive. If they want to live, they have to forgo many things. They also have to leave everything in our hands and move on. For example, they can't afford to stay attached to their home any more, regardless of how long they have lived there. Homeowners have to leave the details of a sale to us. It's important to handle it this way so that there are no loose ends that can be traced to their new location.

In return, witnesses who enter the program get a fresh start in a new place, monthly subsistence payments, and assistance in finding work. We provide each witness with six months of living expenses and three employment opportunities. If they're not working steadily, we terminate the checks. Witnesses with particularly valuable cases sometimes appeal to the Justice Department for ninety-day extensions of these payments and continue to get them. In most cases, however, witnesses take fairly menial jobs and work hard at them. Knowing that their lives depend on their success probably gives them the appropriate motivation. Some job-related motivations, however, were questionable from the start. One witness with a list of robberies in his rap sheet once asked me if we could possibly find him work in a bank. I couldn't believe he asked.

Most witnesses take advantage of the opportunity to go straight. A Justice Department study found that 82 percent of all criminals who enter the program never commit another crime. That doesn't mean they're above asking us to bend the rules for them. When we relocate a family, some parents ask us to make some "minor" tweaks to a child's school records. We have to tell them that we simply cannot change their C student into an A student, regardless of how much their testimony is helping the government.

Some witnesses manage to get into trouble even after we relocate them. Most of the time, they're picked up for traffic violations, drunk driving, or sometimes for drug possession. Whenever this happens, we're contacted. Unless it's a serious charge—such as murder or drug dealing—we work with the local police to have them released into our custody.

Witnesses are full of surprises. Mobsters often ask to have both their families and their girlfriends relocated with them. It's not unusual for them to want separate housing for a mistress they want to continue to see. *WITSEC* mentions one witness I knew who agreed to be relocated only if we promised to obtain breast surgery for his wife.[2] Other witnesses conveniently forget our rules about the necessity of maintaining a low profile. One witness thought that his background qualified him to run for sheriff and another ran for mayor of Austin, Texas. There are sad stories too. One witness was an unfortunate victim in the same plane crash that killed Audie Murphy, the movie star and highly decorated World War II hero.

When preparing my doubles for the TV show, I stressed that not everyone in Witness Protection is a criminal. We are often asked to help people who are in danger for other reasons. I interviewed Frank Serpico, the New York City police officer who testified about the department's widespread payoffs in 1971. His actions launched an inquiry into police corruption by a panel known as the Knapp Commission. Other cops working with Serpico reportedly set him up. While he was entering an apartment during a drug bust, they didn't provide the backup he needed, and the drug dealer shot him. After he recovered from the shooting, he considered entering the program but didn't want to change his identity. Instead he moved to Switzerland.

---

2.   Early and Shur, *WITSEC*, 207.

The program also relocates innocent people who testify as victims or know things that put them in danger. In 1969 hired killers assassinated Joseph Yablonski, his wife, and daughter, after he ran for the presidency of the United Mine Workers Union against an allegedly corrupt union president. Before he was killed Yablonski asked that the Department of Labor investigate the election for fraud. We provided new identities for the two informants who blew the lid off this brutal murder.

Certainly some people have decided not to enter the program. The Justice Department doesn't force anyone to relocate or change his or her identity; it's a personal decision that every witness makes for his or her own safety. There are also people who enter the program and then decide to leave. One mobster was relocated after he testified against the Mafia; then he left the program and wrote a book that became the basis for the movie *Goodfellas*. After Joe Barboza had been in the program for a while, he decided to leave because he thought he was safe. Unfortunately another mobster recognized him while he was in San Francisco and had him killed. The mob had obviously not forgotten about his testimony. Just as we can't force witnesses to enter the program, we can't force them to stay. For most witnesses, remaining in the program is the only way that we can guarantee their safety.

Barboza's case illustrates an important point. The Witness Protection Program has never lost a single witness who followed the program's rules. Since its start in 1970, we've relocated more than 7,500 witnesses and 9,500 family members. That's an impressive reputation. The Marshals Service has also helped other nations to start similar programs. Today there are witness protection programs in Israel and in many European countries that have received training, advice, and support from our experienced team.

Since some witnesses are not used to being law-abiding citizens, there are times when they break our strict rules and have to be removed from the program. For example, one Harlem police officer received kickbacks from drug dealers to look the other way and shared the profits with his sergeant. When he was caught, he agreed to testify. Even after he was accepted into the program, he continued getting into trouble and was eventually sentenced to life in prison. I recall flying with him on his private plane after he joined the program and wondering whether he might try to harm me, but he didn't.

I also remember interviewing the black gangster Frank Lucas about the possibility of entering Witsec. Denzel Washington portrayed Lucas fairly accurately in the movie *American Gangster*. Lucas harmed many people and was a ruthless guy. Eventually he ended up going back to jail for dealing drugs.

Witsec regularly put me in close proximity to hired killers and Mafia hoodlums. In most cases, you wouldn't suspect their occupations by looking at them or talking with them. They appeared quite normal, could be charming and friendly, and often looked for ways to show their appreciation. They were pleasant most of the time. I don't recall ever being treated badly by a witness. They frequently wanted to take us out for dinner. Because the program didn't give them the money they were used to having, we often ended up paying.

Most mob witnesses were extremely family oriented and had large, close-knit families. I'm sure this made it difficult for them to enter the program, as they had to break many of these ties. They were also part of another family—the mob—one they took a blood oath to join. The code they lived by made it possible for them to kill people and show little remorse. It was a strange set of ethics, one that's familiar to anyone who's watched *The Sopranos*.

During a friendly conversation with one mobster I knew well, I wondered how he slept at night. "I don't know how you cope with killing all of those people," I said. His viewpoint was clear. "Louie, keep in mind that I didn't kill anybody that didn't need killing," he said. "We kind of do you guys a favor. We don't kill people unless we really have to; they have to be pretty bad guys. And we always keep it inside; we don't go outside and hurt innocent bystanders."

A killing was usually fast and painless. A small-caliber bullet in the head brought instant death. None of the guys I knew tortured anyone, contrary to what's seen in the movies. If they had to kill you, it was over quickly. They also weren't as careless as today's inner-city gangs. Since mobsters like to think of themselves as businessmen, most of what they did seemed connected with business decisions in some way. In comparison to today's gangs, they were much better organized. They didn't want to draw attention to themselves or do anything that was bad for business. For many years they refused to get involved with drugs because they perceived the drug business as "dirty." Eventually they saw the potential for money and changed their minds, but it was their lower-level associates who primarily handled drugs.

I rarely worried about my own safety when around these men. I treated every witness with respect, and they treated me the same way. Sometimes I wondered if a mobster might decide to come after my family. While I was involved with one of the biggest drug dealers in the Washington, D.C., area, Rayful Edmond, I received a threatening phone call at home one evening. The caller said that if we didn't back off, my family would pay. I immediately contacted the U.S. attorney in Washington, D.C., who began an investigation of the threat. That was the only time I've ever been threatened; nothing ever came of it.

Despite the good relations I had with many witnesses, I never let my guard down. I never forgot that I was dealing with people with criminal tendencies. Witnesses were not above trying to set up a deputy to get themselves additional leverage. They'd try to entice you with favors, including offering to arrange for sex with attractive young ladies. If you accepted, they had you in a compromising position. They were very smart. I don't know of any deputies who were hurt while working with witnesses, but a few had their reputations and their careers damaged.

Some witnesses would do almost anything to keep those monthly checks coming. I once delivered a subsistence check to a female witness. When I knocked at the door, she answered wearing practically nothing. This beautiful young woman began telling me how lonely she was. No one would have to know about us, she said. I knew better and never stepped into the house. Not long after this, I heard about a deputy who was dismissed after he got into a similar situation.

Finding deputies willing to work with witnesses was difficult. Most of us became U.S. marshals because we wanted to arrest criminals. The thought of "babysitting" a killer was often difficult to swallow. Some of the marshals in charge of our districts even refused to have protected witnesses in their jurisdiction. In a few isolated instances, deputies took advantage of witnesses by making them work for them. Because we dealt primarily with the mob, we rarely worked with black witnesses. One of the few times that we did, we learned that one deputy forced the witness and his family to pick cotton. This type of behavior was not tolerated.

It takes a special type of deputy to work in witness protection. This person has to be able to find satisfaction in helping people rather than arresting them. That individual has to treat every witness fairly and not let feelings about witness behavior interfere with this responsibility. There is no room for deputies who think that witnesses are the scum of the earth, who think that we're making a big mistake by not throwing them in prison. More than a few deputies feel that way about witnesses. What they fail to recognize is that witnesses have rather unique problems and offer great opportunities to the law enforcement community.

A witness's life isn't easy. Witnesses who relocate with their families have complex problems. As mentioned earlier, witnesses have to shut the door on their friends, their relatives, and their neighborhoods to stay alive. They don't get the chance to say good-bye. Imagine a witness with a teenage daughter who has just been separated from her boyfriend or with a wife who has never lived apart from her brothers and sisters. Remaining in the danger zone means that everyone's lives are at risk, so we move witnesses and their families quickly once they're accepted into the program. They're in a new area, they're isolated, and the family is often angry and depressed.

One of the hardest parts of working with witnesses is dealing with their children. Most of the kids want to talk to their friends. When they're isolated in a new location, it's even harder for them because they can't fall back on these relationships. They might not want to go to a new school because they don't know anyone. More than once they've called their friends in the old neighborhood to brag. "I'm not in Minnesota anymore. I'm with the U.S. marshals all the time." A call like that provides all the information the mob needs to find a family. Many times the mob watches a kid's friends in order to get information. Other times the kid gets frustrated and runs away. Anything that compromises witnesses' security like this forces us to move them again and provide them with new identities. It can be a frustrating situation for everyone.

Families who are divorced offer other complications. If the parent who is being relocated takes the children, how does the other parent get visitation? How will they learn what's happened to the kids? What about alimony considerations? How will payments be made? Before we can take any action involving the children in these situations, we have to get authorization from a judge.

The witnesses are caught in the middle. They've just agreed to testify against their mob buddies. Now their families are mad at them. The families are having problems and the witnesses are wondering whether they did the right thing. It's our job to reassure them, to convince them that the decision to help the government is the best choice for everyone. "Babying" a witness like this is really a small price to pay if it helps the government's case against crime.

A witness security specialist understands that witnesses can't call their families. We can't allow them to call relatives because we know that the mob has the equipment to trace calls. The mob is smart enough to ask witnesses' friends and family if they've heard from them. To stay alive, witnesses have to stay isolated; that's very hard for most of them. Witnesses go through a lot of inner turmoil.

Sometimes witnesses need rather basic assistance. They're used to buying expensive suits and driving the best cars. Their wives are used to being able to buy nearly anything they want. Suddenly they're living on a small monthly check. It's a situation that's not familiar to them. Many of them need help learning to live on a budget.

Deputies who become witness security specialists understand that they're providing a service to the government by taking care of witnesses. When you understand the big picture, listening to their troubles, acting like a substitute father or a social worker pays off. One witness's testimony can enable us to put many bad guys out of operation and can make a major contribution to law enforcement. It doesn't take much for mistreated, angry witnesses who are under a lot of stress to decide that they're not testifying. We don't want to contribute to this possibility. We want to encourage witnesses to tell the courts what they know. A single testimony is sometimes all that's needed to put fifteen or twenty people in prison.

Because of our expertise in keeping people safe, Witness Protection is often responsible for providing security for prominent witnesses during high-profile trials at the attorney general's request. We don't give these people new identities; we just keep them out of sight and transport them safely to the courtroom. We provided this protection for the activist H. Rap Brown, who was part of the militant Black Panther Party during the late 1960s. Because he failed to appear in court on charges of inciting to riot and carrying a weapon across state lines, he made the FBI's Ten Most Wanted List.

When I was transporting Brown to testify in New Orleans in 1972, I found him to be a fascinating conversationalist, extremely intelligent and likeable. We discussed a wide range of subjects, touching on everything from different societies to world events. He seemed to know about everything. I wondered how he ended up on the wrong side of the tracks.

Instead of taking a commercial flight, we arranged to transport Brown on a Drug Enforcement Agency (DEA) plane. We were engrossed in conversation when we noticed that something strange had happened: The plane's engines had stopped. We looked at each other as this fact sunk in. "Oh man, we're dead," I said, as I jumped up and headed toward the pilot. It turned out that this plane had two gas tanks and the pilot had to momentarily cut the engines while switching to the other one. The pilot apologized over and over for not informing us, but we were just happy that the plane wasn't going to crash.

I enjoyed Rap Brown's company while we were protecting him. Years later I learned that this intelligent, likeable man ended up serving time for armed robbery in New York. It seemed like such a shame.

We also protected Patty Hearst, the granddaughter of the famous publisher William Randolph Hearst, who was kidnapped from her apartment by members of the Symbionese Liberation Army (SLA), an extremist revolutionary group. Hearst, who was originally held for ransom, appeared at a bank robbery two months after her abduction, carrying a rifle as an apparent member of the group. Her kidnapping and trial received much media coverage, particularly since many thought that she had been brainwashed by her captors. We guarded this quiet, attractive lady as she testified in the trials of other SLA members. While she was found guilty for her involvement in the robbery and sentenced to seven years in federal prison, President Carter had her sentence reduced to twenty-one months and President Clinton pardoned her.

We also safeguarded John Hinckley in 1981, while he was on trial for shooting President Reagan, but didn't actually begin this protection until a month or more after the assassination attempt. Nearly every time that I spoke with Hinckley, I wondered how he could have done such as thing. I knew he must have problems, but he often seemed like a normal guy, fairly intelligent with a decent memory. He even showed an interest in how I became a deputy.

When the order to protect Hinckley came, I didn't completely agree with it. While I knew it might be a problem to house him with other prisoners, I didn't fully understand the rationale for this particular detail. I didn't get an explanation. The only answer I got was, "You have to protect him. He tried to kill the president." That response didn't help me; it just raised other questions. "Who are we protecting this guy from?" I wondered. "The Secret Service?"

Without a doubt, our most prominent witnesses were the men from President Richard Nixon's staff indicted for their role in the Watergate scandal. Because of their prominence, we couldn't put them in a regular prison during the highly publicized trial. Instead, we used a special safe house at Fort Holabird, a deserted army base in Maryland, where we sometimes housed other witnesses. We modified one building to make it capable of housing multiple witnesses, made it more secure, and then erected a high fence around it.

At various times during the Watergate trials, we housed men who had been close to the president, so we really had to be on our toes. John Dean had been the White House counsel, Bob Haldeman was Nixon's chief of staff, and Chuck Colson was his chief counsel. We watched them around the clock. We also had G. Gordon Liddy, who had been an FBI agent and was now charged with the burglary that prompted the Watergate investigation. When we picked him up to transport him, he knew the routine before we said anything and quietly put out his hands to be cuffed. He was loyal to Nixon and even said that he was willing to take a bullet for him. With his solid build and tough demeanor, he wasn't someone I ever wanted to tangle with. I remember thinking that if he ever started trouble, we might be forced to shoot him.

Watergate nearly created serious problems for me. Before any of the incidents began, Reis called me into his office to ask me to stay late one evening. He and I had been instructed to wait for a phone call from a contact in the Justice Department and then head to the Howard Johnson hotel across from the Watergate building. The two of us waited and waited at the office, but no call came. Finally, Reis got a call that said we could forget about the assignment.

Later that evening Reis called me at home and excitedly reported that five men were caught breaking into the Watergate building. We were shocked, as well as worried about how we could have been involved. While we had no clear instructions about our intended roles that night, we both thought that we were likely meant to act as lookouts during the burglary.

Things became more complicated. During the investigation, someone must have said something about our supposed involvement. Investigators showed up at our offices, read us both our rights, and began questioning us separately. We both worried that we would be either dismissed or sent to prison. While the investigators said they would be back, we never heard from them again. It amazed us how we nearly got into trouble, even though we were just following our orders and doing our jobs.

In 1978, Witness Protection also safeguarded a prominent witness in what became known as the "Korea Gate" or "Rice Gate" scandal. Tongsun Park, a millionaire from South Korea, was going to testify before Congress about money he had reportedly given to congressmen to influence their decisions to provide aid to his government. There were also questions about his involvement with the Korean intelligence agency.

Since Park was supposed to testify on Capitol Hill, the congressional committee wanted us to keep him safe. I wasn't sure who would try to hurt him at first. We later learned that there were concerns that he might be in danger from other Koreans who wanted to get back at the Korean intelligence agency. Together with an FBI agent named Al Meyers, I traveled to Korea to escort Park safely to the United States. We had a layover in Hawaii after the flight from Korea. Since our assignment was supposed to be as low profile as possible, we did our best to conceal Park. Despite our efforts, the front page of the *Honolulu Star* carried a picture of the three of us at the airport.

Park didn't seem concerned about remaining out of sight. While we were in Hawaii, he wanted to eat at the best restaurants. We knew that neither the FBI nor the Marshals Service would be happy about us eating at these places, but somehow we managed. We justified our meals by saying that it enabled us to ensure Park's safety. Thankfully the government picked up the tab.

On the flight home, I was amazed at how often Park changed clothes. He must have gone through three or four wardrobe changes. He was also quite a drinker. As long as it didn't cause problems, we let him down glass after glass of vodka tonic. His behavior certainly confirmed his reputation as the "Asian Great Gatsby," a man who was famous for the dinner parties he threw in Washington to influence congressmen. Once we reached the Washington, D.C., area, Park was housed in a safe site for the duration of his testimony. A beautiful blonde who lived in the Watergate complex frequently visited him.

It's common knowledge that the Secret Service is charged with protecting the president, the vice president, their families, and candidates for the White House. When other prominent government officials require protection, the responsibility typically goes to the witness security specialists within the Marshals Service. The attorney general's office sometimes asks for our help in these situations.

When Ted Kennedy's life was threatened, we protected the senator and his family for about a month, until the threat was investigated and closed. To ensure his safety, our deputies accompanied him to the Senate building and escorted his family wherever they went. This included taking frequent trips with the senator to McDonald's. He always ordered a burger and fries but sometimes didn't have any cash on him. When this happened, we'd pay for his meal.

Before he ran for president, we also provided similar protection for the senator's brother Robert. In this case, we stayed close to his home and spent many days providing protection for his family. Both of the Kennedy brothers were warm and friendly. Despite how well known they were, they were very down-to-earth people. They didn't seem to be overly impressed with their own wealth and their position. Their wives were also extremely nice to us and made sure that we always had enough to eat. The whole family was always extremely considerate of us; they made us feel like we were important, and it made quite an impression on me.

Robert's boys, however, were particularly mischievous. I was working with another deputy named Hank Johnson one day. Johnson, who was wearing a nice suit, somehow was pushed into the pool by one of the Kennedy boys. One of the other boys found a clever way to get back at me for something I must have done to offend him. When we took Robert and this particular son to the Justice Department one day, I held the door open for them. As the younger Kennedy walked by me in the doorway, he paused just long enough to kick me in the shins. He knew he was safe because he was with his dad. The boys also picked up on my fear of snakes. Because we worked in shifts, the family provided us with a couch where we could sleep in the basement. After one nap, I awoke with a strange feeling. Looking around in the dark, my eyes focused on one Kennedy boy standing over me with a live snake around his neck. I nearly had a heart attack.

We also provided protection for Lyndon Johnson, which was a very different experience from working with the Kennedys. One Thanksgiving we were providing security at his house in Washington, D.C. Everyone was inside having dinner while we remained outside on this particularly cold day. There were no invitations to come in and warm up and no sandwiches. We were given some hot coffee, but we always remained on the outside.

While I may have been an expert at protecting witnesses, dealing with affairs of the heart was a different matter. I've always made friends easily, but I have never dated much. After my troubled first marriage, I promised myself that I'd never get involved again. Thankfully, a sweet and lovely young woman turned me around.

As the program's staff grew, Witness Security was spread out over a couple of floors, which meant that I frequently traveled out of my immediate office area. I couldn't help but notice one particular woman who worked down the hall, and I often remarked to myself that she was probably the prettiest woman that I'd ever seen. Every time I saw her, my resolve weakened. When I finally got up the nerve to speak to her and we eventually began seeing each other, I slowly started becoming more optimistic.

While I enjoyed talking with Judy, at first I didn't think that anything else would develop. I knew that we were both cautious about dating someone in the office, and I was particularly skittish because of my pending divorce. When I realized that I had real feelings for Judy, I was somewhat torn. I thought that she probably was interested in me only as a friend or that she felt sorry for me. One day I asked her if she needed a ride home. When she said no, I stayed away from her for quite a while, thinking that I'd made a fool of myself. The next time she bumped into me, she asked why I'd stayed away. The only reason she said no to my offer of a ride was because she had already had one.

During the long assignment at Wounded Knee, I frequently spoke about various work-related matters to someone who worked near Judy. I always asked her to tell Judy that I said hello. When I returned, we continued talking, and I eventually got up the nerve to ask her out. The first time that I actually kissed her goodnight, I thought that I'd died and gone to heaven. I knew that I'd fallen in love. In spite of my own intentions, love had found me and brought the two of us together. When my divorce was finalized, Judy and I were married in a small civil ceremony. Just after the ceremony, we newlyweds found a parking ticket on my windshield. Even that couldn't cloud this happy day or our future.

When a husband works in law enforcement, it can create a lot of stress for his wife, as she typically worries that he might be killed on the job. Many marriages can't handle this additional stress. Often a spouse will turn to alcohol to cope, or the marriage will simply end in divorce. I've been so blessed to have such an understanding and supportive spouse. Judy has always told me that if I'm happy with my work, then she's happy. Whenever I've had to travel on assignments, she's asked to know only that I'm safe. As long as I call regularly to let her know that I'm OK, everything is fine. She deserves a lot of credit because I know it hasn't been an easy road.

During the preparation for the TV game show appearance, I said nothing about the people we were protecting, for obvious reasons. In addition, I did not mention the negative publicity that surrounded Witsec.

People across the country were shocked and worried, primarily because of the 1977 publication of *The Alias Program* by Fred Graham. When the public learned from this book that the government was hiding convicted criminals under new identities, everyone worried that we had relocated these people to their own neighborhoods. When the media learned that some witnesses committed murders even after they were relocated, Congress began public hearings in 1978 to further investigate Witsec and calm everyone down.

Surprisingly, it was the program's early success that created many of these problems. During our first few years we were a shoestring operation working with only a handful of witnesses. In less than ten years the number of witnesses shot up to more than four hundred, despite our limited manpower and even more limited budget.

As the program continued expanding, Witsec began moving away from its original mission, which was providing protection for people whose lives were in danger because of their testimony. Somehow we began ignoring the program's acceptance criteria and started taking people who didn't testify or were involved in cases that had little effect on major federal or state efforts against organized crime or drug traffickers. It seemed like everyone was jumping on the bandwagon. The influx of new witnesses was stretching our already strained program beyond its limits.

Getting anything accomplished was like running an obstacle course. There were many times that we had to create important documents for witnesses without the proper authorization, simply because we lacked the appropriate contacts in other agencies. We were chronically short-staffed, which meant that many of us also worked weekends and overtime to protect witnesses. These around-the-clock details were a strain on everyone's family life.

We even had problems getting support from our own districts. There were many times when I got on the phone and begged a district to loan us a deputy to help with a witness. Just as many times, the district declined.

Because balancing the concerns of the Justice Department, the U.S. attorneys, and our own operation was no easy feat, finding someone to lead this complex program in those early days was problematic. Not many of the people who started leading our operation lasted more than a few months. Not surprisingly, fourteen marshals came and went during this period, according to the count in *WITSEC*, as though the leadership role had its own revolving door.[3] Because we were having organizational and operational issues, other federal agencies became hesitant to send witnesses to us. Even our own director seemed to keep our operation at arm's length, emphasizing that the primary mission of the Marshals Service was to support the federal courts and deal with civil disturbances. Morale in Witsec was at an all-time low.

Things began to change for us when William Hall became deputy director for the Marshals Service. Hall brought in Reis Kash to run our operation. Reis's background in military intelligence enabled him to organize Witsec quickly and make some critical improvements. He helped to establish better criteria for anyone entering the program and gave us more of a say in the witness acceptance process. Prior to this, we were forced to take anyone the Justice Department sent. Obtaining the Justice Department's agreement to improve this process gave us the opportunity to evaluate witnesses, make risk assessments, and provide our input before anyone was accepted for relocation. This change not only enforced the strict acceptance criteria that had been instituted, it increased the cooperation and communication between the marshals and the Justice Department. Giving our people a say in the acceptance process improved our status and gave us new authority. We were no longer just hired hands or security guards. Our opinions began to matter.

Not long after Reis made these changes, I was transferred to the Marshals' internal affairs group and left the operation for two years. The deputies running internal affairs thought that my law-enforcement background and investigative experience could be helpful in investigations we regularly conducted into the conduct of our deputies. During the time that I was reassigned, Witsec got yet another new leader, Art Daniels, who continued revitalizing the organization. Art asked me to return as one of two deputies reporting to him with responsibility for the entire operation. Jim O'Toole ran the administrative side of Witsec, with responsibility for budgets, equipment, witness-related paperwork, and similar details. Because of my history with the program, Art asked me to head the operations unit, where I would be responsible for the fieldwork involved in protecting and relocating witnesses. It was a very efficient set up.

---

3.   Early and Shur, *WITSEC*, 159.

Art had cleaned house in Witsec. Fresh and eager college-educated people replaced the older deputies who seemed to be biding their time until retirement. Most of these new people worked directly with witnesses in the field. I worked closely with the specialists, putting them on new assignments and making sure that they had whatever they needed. Whenever a witness needed to be transported to court or relocated, I dispatched a detail there and organized the shifts needed to provide twenty-four-hour protection. We eventually had more than a hundred specialists working with witnesses. Unlike during my previous stint with Witsec, we certainly weren't starved for resources. While handling scheduling and overtime sounds like a real headache, I found that I had a knack for this work. While I'd always liked working directly with the witnesses, my new position was just as enjoyable. I especially loved interacting with the specialists and paying periodic visits to help with any problems.

Witsec has always had great people, even before this influx of new deputies. The program would not have survived its formative years if we hadn't. Some of the deputies who worked within the program were beyond great. It's no stretch to call some of them legendary.

John Partington, who led the detail that protected Joe "the Animal" Barboza, was one of the first deputies to safeguard a Mafia witness and his family. John made such significant contributions to our operation that I think he deserves the name, "Mr. Witness Security."

There was something special about John, who displayed a rare and instinctive talent for anything related to dealing with witnesses. He could always get the necessary documents and knew how to handle the most troublesome guys. No one could get a witness to cooperate like John could; he had a way of bringing them around. Sometimes he seemed to get a little too close to the witnesses, but interacting with people like this was part of his nature. Working with him was an education; just watching him taught me a lot.

John could organize an efficient protection detail, deal with the demands of the U.S. attorney's office, and always remained a great role model for other deputies. He wasn't the type of leader who only told others what to do. If we told him about something that needed to be done, typically he'd do it himself. I can't say enough about John; he was a gifted deputy.

There were other stellar deputies working in Witsec. Frank Anderson made great contributions to the program, as did Steve Millinger, who used to play for the Washington Redskins.

Howard Safir, who eventually became New York City's police commissioner under Mayor Rudolph Giuliani in 1996, took the entire Witsec operation to the next level. It's fair to say that he revolutionized Witsec. Howard was originally loaned to the Marshals Service from DEA for only a year, but ended up staying longer. He became instrumental in computerizing Witsec, putting everything we needed to know about a witness at our fingertips. He refined our policies, guidelines, and regulations, organizing them for easy reference for anyone who had questions. In addition to the technology, he improved the network of safe sites used to house witnesses.

Under Howard's leadership, Witsec was freed from a major structural weakness. Previously the deputies interested in working as witness security specialists continued reporting to the marshal in their local district, where we had to compete for their attention against other assignments. Howard arranged for these people to focus only on witness-related matters and report directly to us. Being a witness security specialist became a distinct specialization within the Marshals Service, a change that improved the entire operation. This motivated our hardworking deputies and continued to elevate the program's reputation.

Howard also pushed Witsec beyond our work with mob witnesses. Experts came in to regularly provide us with thorough training in dignitary protection. Before long we were providing security for foreign diplomats whenever the United Nations General Assembly met at the UN headquarters in New York. Our elite, specialized unit continues doing this work today.

Being with mob killers for days rarely affected me. When I walked out on stage for *To Tell the Truth* and saw the cameras and a studio full of people, however, I was nervous. No one told me that there'd be an audience at the taping of our show; I thought the laughter was dubbed in later. Apparently, when word filtered out that there'd be an episode about the Witness Protection Program, people started filling up the room.

Somehow I managed to hold it together through the program. The panelists peppered the three of us with questions, trying to pick the two imposters.
When it came time for them to announce their guesses, everyone selected the
same guy, contestant number two, who really worked in an executive placement company. No one picked me.

At the end of the program, the emcee said, "Will the real Louie McKinney please stand up?" When I did, everyone was surprised. Someone in the
audience began shouting and causing a ruckus. When the noisy man in the audience stood up, I could tell that he'd been drinking. He was telling everyone
how great it was that no one thought that the real witness security specialist
was a black man, like him. As he was escorted from the building, I could hear
him yelling, "Right on, brother."

Race had nothing to do with the outcome. When my boss, Jack, picked me
to participate in this popular TV show, he wasn't thinking about putting the
grown son of a southern sharecropper on TV. He wasn't scheming about having a farm boy raised in the South on a popular prime-time program.

When Jack picked me, he told everyone, "If anyone can fool these guys,
Louie can." Jack picked me because I was a witness security specialist. He
picked me because I knew something about changing identities.

9
Deputy in Paradise
Rising through the Ranks in the U.S. Virgin Islands

I've been to paradise. Actually, it's probably more accurate to say that I've been to "America's paradise," a name frequently used to describe the U.S. Virgin Islands. At different times during my career, I lived on the island of St. Thomas and can confirm that "paradise" is a very accurate description. Our home provided a breathtaking view of beautiful Magens Bay, we swam in sparkling, clear water at pristine beaches, and we visited historic places like Blackbeard's Castle, which still cause us all to marvel.

My career with the Marshals Service had its share of trips to grim prisons and weeks spent guarding criminals at remote safe houses. By contrast, it's also enabled me to take my family to many fabulous places, places that a country boy from South Carolina never imagined in his wildest dreams.

My first glimpse of this island paradise came during the 1972 trial of the Fountain Valley Five. This group of heavily armed men boldly entered the clubhouse of the Fountain Valley Golf Course, located on the island of St. Croix, on September 6, 1972. Before escaping into the rainforest, these native islanders shot and killed eight people, including four U.S. tourists. Because the islands are a U.S. territory, any crimes committed there are considered federal offenses, which is why the Marshals Service became involved. In the aftermath of the murders, our deputies worked on this case. Less than a week later, all five men had been found, arrested, and charged after an intensive search. After a lengthy deliberation, the local jury found the suspects guilty of murder, as well as multiple counts of assault and robbery.

I was working with the Marshals' internal affairs group at the time and was sent to look into the actions of some of the people we had involved in the trial, as there were accusations that our deputies were getting too close to members of the jury, whom they were sequestering. There were reports that the deputies and jurists were out together in public. Not only was this type of fraternization unprofessional, it could result in a mistrial. Because of the role that I played in "policing the police," neither the local deputies I investigated nor the jurors I questioned were happy to see me. The deputies even referred to me as the "headhunter." I wasn't out to get anyone fired, though. My only concern was that we were doing things the right way. Despite my good intentions, here I was on this beautiful island paradise and no one wanted anything to do with me.

Six years later, in 1978, the service's deputy director approached me about going to the Virgin Islands as chief deputy, which is considered quite an honor. Outside of being appointed one of the country's ninety-five U.S. marshals, the role of chief deputy is the highest position that a deputy can attain. Once again I struggled with the thought of leaving my role in headquarters for a new one, even though this new position brought prestige. Our deputy director told me that the service needed someone in the Virgin Islands with good people skills who could solve problems, which were talents that I'd already demonstrated. My ability to work well with people would come in handy in dealing with the islanders, who were frequently resentful of outsiders. To motivate me to accept the job, the service flew me to St. Thomas to look around for a week and get acquainted with our operation. It was as gorgeous as I remembered it from my first trip there in 1972.

Once I accepted the position, my wife, Judy, found a realtor and went house hunting on St. Thomas. It didn't take her long to find the right place. The house, which was owned by the University of the Virgin Islands, sat on a beautiful site on the top of a hill. Its wraparound porch gave us a bird's eye view of every ship that sailed into the nearby harbor. The trees that surrounded the house kept it cool on the hottest days, and the sea breezes made the backyard feel like it was air-conditioned.

Making the transition to chief deputy, however, wasn't as simple as finding a house. There were weeks of specialized training at the federal law-enforcement training center near Atlanta, Georgia, where we were given management training. The class immediately pushed us into new ways of thinking, honing in on every aspect of the administrative and supervisory skills that we would need. Introducing ourselves to the rest of the class required drawing a picture that represented our agency and our role. The rest of the students would use these clues to deduce what we did. Never much of an artist, I approached the board rather nervously when my turn came. Connecting with some long-hidden talent, I quickly sketched a man wearing a gun and gave him a hat with a star. I drew an island for him to stand on, complete with a couple of palm trees, and added the feathered headdress worn by Indian chiefs.

The class pondered what it meant. Finally, someone guessed. "I know what you are," one man said. "You're the chief deputy for the Virgin Islands." Another student, a complete stranger, looked at me and said, "You must be pretty good; you really got your point across." No one suspected that I had no idea what I was doing. I'm still not sure how I came up with that idea. This brief exercise encouraged us to think outside the box, as well as to explore new ways of communicating ideas, both of which would prove valuable in our new roles.

The class was tough, providing us with detailed requirements for handling people, administrative procedures, contracts, and office accounting. Moving to this level of management after working as a deputy is extremely challenging. Several people in my session were there for the second time. I often worried that I wouldn't get a passing grade on the final exam, but I did. I was proud of myself and even thought that I knew everything there was to know about being a chief deputy. I quickly learned that I was mistaken.

A chief deputy is a Marshal's chief of staff. This person has to be an effective manager of people, an efficient administrator, and a decent bookkeeper. He or she is solely responsible for all the paperwork that comes out of the office: the monthly reports, the details about how funds were spent, and everything else that requires a signature. I'd never signed my name so many times. Every month I filled out the required paperwork and sent what we called a "ten pack," which accounted for ten categories of financial expenditures, to the Justice Department. The job itself was a crash course in administration, something with which I had little experience.

The attitude of my administrative support person made getting through the paperwork even more challenging. There were seven people working in the district office in St. Thomas when I arrived. Some of them, including this administrative officer, harbored resentment, simply because I was an outsider. She even tried to trip me up by making mistakes in the reports to see if I would catch them. She didn't understand why the service brought in someone from Washington, D.C., rather than give the job to someone already in the office. Since she was accustomed to doing things her way, she initially resisted any changes to accommodate me. After we worked together for a few months and she got to know me better, she owned up about her attitude. One day she said that she initially felt I looked down on her because she was an islander. She saw that she'd been wrong about me and even confessed to the errors she planted in the paperwork.

There's more to being a chief deputy than paperwork; I was also responsible for supervising the ten to fourteen deputies working within the district. In the Virgin Islands, that meant overseeing people on St. Thomas, St. Croix, and St. John. Unfortunately, we didn't have the manpower that we needed to cover those areas because no one had examined the operation closely enough to justify the additional help. Because we were understaffed, I often had to handle some duties myself, including taking prisoners to court. This rarely happens to chief deputies in the States; they're able to take more of a management role and focus on the issues that Marshals Service headquarters might deem important. They even have supervisors to whom they can delegate various responsibilities. I had to do everything myself, from handling staffing concerns in the court and making sure warrants were served to managing prisoner transportation.

My outsider status made investigations difficult. The islands were a close-knit community of people living on relatively small land areas. Asking islanders for information on a crime was like asking them to turn in family members. Not everyone was related, but on an island like St. Thomas, which is only twelve miles long and three miles wide, everyone seems to know everyone else.

When we arrested a bank robber in St. Thomas around 1978, it was the first time that one of these crimes was solved. People actually cried because we had arrested someone they knew. We had difficulty keeping them away from him while we were transporting him to jail and to trial and were eventually forced to remove him from the island.

Regardless of the crime, islanders always seemed to stick together and protect their own. Even the local police seemed to have difficulty solving cases. One of the immigration judges was stabbed numerous times during a robbery attempt while walking from his office to a local hotel. Since I was relatively new at the time, I agreed to let the police take charge of the investigation. Even after two or three months, they couldn't seem to produce any leads. Because the judge died, the lack of progress worried me, as I knew that the killer was probably still on the island. Once we took over the investigation, we located the murderer—the brother of one of the local cops—within a week.

I didn't know if I could completely trust the local police at the time. Sometimes, when we gave them advance warning of a raid, the places that we raided were empty, leading us to believe that the people we were looking for had been warned. While I'm sure that not all of them were corrupt, quite a few officers were arrested while I was on the islands. In the aftermath of Hurricane Hugo, some of them even participated in looting food, appliances, and other items from local stores. The Marshals' Special Operations Group had to be called in to restore order. Eventually a change in leadership in 1980 transformed the local police into the professional force it is today. The new commissioner enabled the department to obtain vehicles and equipment that put it on a par with other police units and provided the training needed to increase professional standards. I remain good friends with the police commissioner and know many good officers in what is now an exemplary department.

Paradise never comes without difficulty. On my first shopping trip in the islands, I went to a local grocery store to buy some meat, milk, and a few other small items. The cashier rang up my purchase and said, "That will be ninety-eight dollars." "Wait a minute, miss," I answered. "That can't be; I don't have that much stuff. Are you sure you didn't add someone else's bill together with mine?" The cashier calmly called the manager, and I repeated my statements to him. As he quoted the price of each item, he added them up as I watched. The cashier was right. I had no idea that the cost of living was that high. I'd only bought a few items and could carry my expensive groceries home in one hand. I later learned that while there were no price controls on food, the local markets offered bargain prices on gold, perfume, and alcoholic beverages.

There wasn't much I could do about the prices, but I did make considerable progress on overcoming my outsider status. I began attending community meetings, going to the middle schools and high schools, and talking to people in various organizations. I let them all know that I was there to help. Things began turning around once I began hiring some of the local police and corrections officers from the prisons as guards. When they weren't working a regular shift, I paid them to help us transport prisoners between the jail and the courts. Eventually, I was invited to speak at the island's police academy. After a while, people began greeting me in the street and became more cooperative. When I needed help in solving a crime, I was usually given the necessary information.

We made good friends while we lived in the islands. In my work, I became friendly with other people working in law enforcement, including other federal agents, the police commissioner, and captains on the local force. I also socialized with people in other important roles, including lawyers, teachers, and even the governor. Since I'm a friendly person by nature, I also became close to people who did work on my house, the cashier at the grocery store, and a variety of other folks I still communicate with regularly. When I had to travel back to the States, I felt safe leaving my family, knowing that our friends would look after them if they needed anything. I've always made it a point to treat people with respect. I never look down on anyone, even people that I have to arrest. Some of the Americans who operated the big restaurants, boats, and hotels seemed very class conscious and tended to look down on the poorer island people. That attitude doesn't get you far. Everyone deserves to be treated with respect.

Since St. Thomas is the first port of entry into the United States, the islands in the vicinity had a problem with illegal aliens. It's always been common for people to move between the U.S. Virgin Islands and their British, French, or Dutch counterparts. With approximately thirty other islands in such close proximity—including Puerto Rico and Guadeloupe—it's easy to stow away on any ship and get smuggled to another island destination. People who want to live in this U.S. territory can easily find others who are willing to sell them the necessary documents—such as a driver's license—to make them appear to be citizens. Finding ways to prevent illegal immigration is difficult, especially since it's been going on for so many years. Once people got in, finding and deporting them was difficult. Eventually the U.S. attorney and the immigration office on the islands assembled a team of immigration specialists and made it a crime to immigrate illegally; the punishment for this crime was deportation.

The island's drug trade also kept us quite busy, with routine shipments of marijuana, cocaine, and heroin passing through the area. Scotland Yard once informed us about a boat coming from England that was reportedly carrying a large shipment. We waited until the British crew docked and then boarded it, seizing both the drugs and the luxurious boat transporting this illegal cargo. Because it was used to transport drugs, we eventually sold the expensive vessel in an auction. We didn't get what it was worth, but we turned the funds over to the U.S. Treasury, where the money was put to good use.

In addition to using the local police for prisoner transport duties, I also increased the number of deputies. When I arrived, there were only four or five deputies each in St. Thomas and St. Croix. Less than two years later we had nearly four times as many. Getting the new positions was a matter of being the "squeaky wheel." I regularly let headquarters understand how shorthanded the district was. In addition to regular calls and letters, I also enlisted the help of one of the local federal judges, who expressed his concerns to the Justice Department. Not long after the judge's communication, the personnel office sent people to evaluate our operation, and they saw that we clearly needed more help. I began hiring as soon as I got the authorization and employed a number of qualified islanders, in addition to bringing in some deputies from the States.

Because the district wasn't part of the mainland, its equipment needs had also been virtually ignored. I knew that it was a case of "out of sight, out of mind," and that rationale didn't cut it. We had no cars, which forced deputies serving process or executing warrants to perform this duty while riding bicycles, something they didn't seem to question. I began modernizing the operation, obtaining computers, office furniture, and vehicles. This greatly improved my reputation with the deputies and the people working in the office, of course, but I did it because I saw no reason why we should have fewer resources than the districts in the States.

I also developed good working relationships with the other federal agencies that worked on the islands. Initially we were drawn together because we were outsiders. While there's often a rivalry between the FBI and the Marshals Service, the agents in the Virgin Islands were extremely helpful and friendly. Together with agents from the DEA and ATF working on St. Thomas and St. Croix, we developed a tradition of information sharing. We convened every month to learn about the various areas within the islands and to meet the local officials. I arranged our transportation with the captain at the Coast Guard station, who provided a cutter to take us where we wanted to go. We went to Aruba, Curasol, Trinidad, Tobago, and other islands. We'd meet with the police chief or the police commissioner, have lunch, and share information. We discussed the unsolved crimes being investigated, actions under way to proactively prevent problems, and what we knew about the local drug trafficking operations

Knowing the right person to call helped me enormously. For example, we were hunting for a fugitive who I suspected was hiding in Martinique. Since that island belongs to France, we'd normally have to contact the French authorities to arrange for extradition. Instead of following this lengthy process and giving the fugitive more time to escape, I now could call the local police. All they had to do was kick the fugitive off the island, since he was there illegally, and put him on a boat for St. Thomas, where we'd be waiting for him.

Instituting this partnership with federal and local officials also provided us with a degree of security. We all knew that if a crisis developed—whether it was a protest, a riot, or a natural disaster—there would be a delay of about six hours until help arrived from the mainland. By sticking together, we had a better chance of coming out on top.

During one of our monthly meetings, we had some unexpected excitement. A group of us were on a Coast Guard vessel headed for one of these regular gatherings on Virgin Gorda, which is part of the British Virgin Islands, when the captain received a call for a search-and-rescue effort. I recall being with FBI, ATF, and DEA agents on the ship that day, together with people from the Immigration and Naturalization Service (INS), the Department of the Interior, and the U.S. attorney's office. These rescue calls always take top priority, so we immediately changed course to help the ship that was in trouble. Because this cutter had a top speed of thirteen knots (or fifteen miles per hour), we ended up at sea for two days, taking a day to reach the ship near San Juan and another day to come back. The vessel's cook made a great meal of steak with rice and beans, but no one wanted to eat, as many in our group became seasick. The FBI agents and the U.S. attorney were hanging over the side of the boat feeling miserable. Luckily, as a former navy man, I wasn't affected.

The boat we went to help was headed to San Juan and had run aground near Anquilla. The Coast Guard was refused when they asked for permission to come aboard. Because we were in international waters, the captain of the other vessel could exercise this right. The vessel's crew said they'd be fine and would wait for the tide to come in and free them. Given their situation, this behavior seemed somewhat strange to everyone. We stayed with them until the boat got free and then followed them to San Juan. Once the boat reached port, we discovered that it was transporting drugs, which explained why the crew hadn't welcomed the Coast Guard.

The Witness Protection Program also provided me with some unexpected excitement in 1980. Witsec inspectors had a demanding and troublesome, high-profile witness, named Jimmy Fratianno, whom they wanted to hide in the islands. Jimmy, who was nicknamed "the Weasel" as a boy, was the highest-ranking mob informant that the government had up until that time.

After three decades in the Mafia, he knew most of the crime bosses in the country and had testified in many trials, while also frequently pushing Witness Protection's strict rules to the limit. Because of his behavior, the program needed to put him somewhere where no one could find him. Since I'd worked in the program, they thought that I'd be the right person to take care of him. From what I'd learned about Jimmy from my contacts in Witness Protection, he liked to be seen, to brag about himself, and to socialize. He'd even done an interview with a television station, something that witnesses are not permitted to do. Initially I worried about my ability to keep him hidden. The guys in the program eventually convinced me that we could make it work.

I met Jimmy, his wife, and his wife's sister at the airport and got them settled in a place that we'd located. I'm not sure how he managed it, but Jimmy, obviously still worried about the mob's threat on his life, had a gun on him. I explained that the Witness Protection Program was responsible for his safety, and somehow he trusted me enough to surrender the gun.

I'd given Jimmy a phone number where he could reach me, something we always did for witnesses. He called all the time, simply because he was used to being around people and wanted company. He was in a new place where he didn't know anyone and gravitated toward me. One day he said that he was going to make me the best lasagna that I'd ever had. He must have spent a long time preparing it. When I sat down with him to eat, it looked and smelled wonderful. Since I hadn't known him very long, I immediately worried that he might try to poison me and waited for him to take the first bite. Satisfied when nothing happened to him, I dug in. It was the best lasagna I've ever had.

The most difficult aspect of having Jimmy in the islands was keeping his identity hidden, which included keeping him away from the deputies. At that point, I still wasn't completely certain about who could be trusted and was taking the necessary precautions to protect this witness. Unfortunately this meant that I sometimes had to make up stories, which I didn't like doing.

Jimmy made things more difficult. Even though I told him that he should never come to my office, he showed up fairly regularly. When people asked who he was, I told them he was with the Justice Department. Since the people in the islands didn't know much about witness protection, they never suspected a thing.

Because the marshal was also a local, I didn't disclose Jimmy's identity to him either. When I had to take Jimmy to the States to testify, the marshal asked why I was traveling so frequently. "Headquarters needed me for a couple of things," I'd say. "They're paying the travel expenses; it's not costing the office any money." That explanation seemed to satisfy him, but being in such a compromising position was difficult for me.

When Jimmy's testimony landed him on the cover of *Newsweek* magazine early in 1981, someone in the office thought they had recognized him from one of his visits. I managed to play dumb and said that the person on the cover looked nothing like the person they remembered. The next day Jimmy showed up in the office again, waving the magazine. "Hey, Louie, they printed a profile about me," he said. "Look at this. Don't I look good?" I didn't say anything. I knew that it was time to pack Jimmy up and move him somewhere else to keep him safe.

I continued hearing about Jimmy even after we relocated him. My sister Elsie was flying from Washington, D.C., to South Carolina and found herself in a conversation with the man sitting next to her, who turned out to be Jimmy. When she told him her name, he asked if she was related to anyone in the Marshals Service. Of course, Elsie mentioned me. According to Elsie, Jimmy couldn't stop talking about me. He even called me the best friend that he's ever had. Thankfully he didn't reveal his association with Witness Protection.

Jimmy was in and out of the program for years. He'd become bothered about something and leave, or he'd be dismissed for breaking rules. When Jimmy found himself missing someone, he didn't hesitate to pick up the phone and call them, even though witnesses are forbidden to make contact with family or friends. But then he'd cut another deal with the U.S. attorneys by revealing new information about the mob that would help them prosecute a case. They also moved him around a lot to keep him alive or to satisfy his whims. Jimmy lived to an old age and was always quite a character. He died peacefully in his sleep in 1993.

Island living appealed to my family, especially to my wife. We were regular visitors to Magens Bay, which *National Geographic* has rated one of the world's top beaches, and we named our daughter after this lovely place. Like my wife, she always loved going to the beach, which makes her name even more appropriate. All of us enjoyed watching the Rastafarians braid their dreadlocks in the bay's saltwater. They stuck to a rigid vegetarian diet but smoked marijuana, supposedly because it aided their prayer and meditation. Many of them took the banana leaves from our trees to smoke for similar purposes.

After nearly two years as chief deputy, I was ready for a change. While I had no real complaints, I was getting restless. Even though I'd added deputies to our staff, we always had more work than we could handle. I was still doing much more than my peers in the States. Having lived in larger metropolitan areas, I was becoming bored with visiting the beach and found myself missing the many activities that are available in big cities. When I received orders to return to the mainland, I was ready to go.

I was proud of what I'd accomplished while working in the islands. I'd made inroads by hiring the first female deputy in our district. I outfitted our deputies with equipment that was comparable to that used by deputies in the States. Many of them had their first opportunity to leave the islands while I was there, as I'd send them on special assignments to New York, Chicago, and San Francisco. Their involvement in extradition cases, witness protection activities, and other assignments expanded their horizons and let them see how law enforcement operated in other places. When they found out that I was leaving, many of them were upset.

Even after stepping down as chief deputy, I didn't stay away from the islands for long. In 1993 the director of the Marshals Service asked me to take over as the district's U.S. marshal. I was replacing Marshal Mel Carter, who had taken my place as chief deputy and went on to become the island's top man within the Marshals Service. Unfortunately Mel developed cancer and medical complications made it necessary for him to resign. Because I was familiar with the workings of the district, the attorney general endorsed me as Mel's replacement. I hesitated to go back again but didn't want to refuse a request from the attorney general. My conversation with Mel convinced me that I should do whatever was in my power to help out my friend.

My role as marshal was more political than that of the chief deputy. While a chief runs the office, the marshal is more externally focused. I was constantly in meetings, shaking hands with various officials, handling public speaking chores, and focusing on getting the funds that we needed to run the district. Because we were still short-staffed, I also pitched in on prisoner transportation and other duties, even though I was now the man in charge. I enjoyed being the guy running the show, as this was the first time in my career that I didn't report directly to someone else.

Despite the heavy workload, I was proud of what we accomplished during my tour as marshal. One job that Mel left unfinished was the organization of a warrant squad, something that I was able to complete for him during my tenure. Together with the DEA, ATF, and other agencies, we were participants in a major drug bust called Operation Sunrise. This operation took a long time to organize—between getting the necessary warrants issued, preparing everyone, and getting additional help from the States—but the results made it worthwhile. The raids we executed before dawn surprised our targets, reduced drug sales among the locals, hurt some big drug traffickers, and made it harder to use the island ports as a stepping-stone to enter the United States. The publicity in the islands that followed the operation made me even happier, since it sent the bad guys a message that we were serious. I also made it clear that regardless of who committed a crime, the law would always be enforced. We arrested local police officers and customs officials who were on the take. Corruption was not tolerated on my watch.

I also arranged the regular transfer of federal prisoners on the islands to stateside prisons, which helped to free up the limited jail space we had available. That might sound like an easy feat, but it required months of negotiations and conversations with headquarters. I knew that planes regularly took prisoners from San Juan, but they never seemed to venture our way. I took a chance and asked, something that apparently no one had done before. After many calls to various offices, I finally made the right connection. When I was told the plane would arrive the following Friday, I couldn't wait. Right on schedule, a big 727 aircraft flew into St. Thomas. The islanders watched as we marched a hundred prisoners in orange jumpsuits onto this heavily guarded plane. Despite some problems with those who hated seeing family members shipped off to federal prisons in the States, the newspaper and TV coverage was positive.

My family has always enjoyed living on and visiting the islands. On this trip both of my children were enrolled in a private school in Antilles. Because of my job, we thought this would offer a safer environment than the local schools. The tuition was pricey, as many wealthy American and European families sent their children to this school. My son, who was about eleven years old, recalls having a difficult time being the new kid. He overcame these difficulties and was overjoyed to visit his island friends again as a graduation present after he finished college.

Sadly, on one of our return visits, we discovered that a hurricane had demolished the beautiful home we had lived in that had offered us so many memorable views of the bay. The frame was standing, but the rest of the structure was in shambles. Like so many other things, construction in the islands is an expensive proposition.

After eighteen months, my family and I returned to the States, ending my first appointment as marshal for the Virgin Islands. However, my career in the islands wasn't over yet. During President Bill Clinton's administration, I received a second appointment. When the attorney general called to ask me to consider this subsequent term, I had already retired from the Marshals Service. Since a marshal's appointment comes directly from the president, not having an active status with the service didn't matter. The attorney general said that my help was needed because the position was vacant and there was concern about the low morale among the deputies in the district.

My appointment was quickly confirmed, and the attorney general's office arranged for me to be promptly sworn in by a federal judge. Since it was near the Christmas holidays, the only judge we could find was in Camden, New Jersey. Together with Judy and my friend Mark Ferris, we took the train north so I could be sworn in. Once the official requirements were fulfilled, I waited until after the first of the year to actually move to the islands again. Although I was told that I'd be filling in for only a few months until a permanent replacement could be found, I ended up staying another eighteen months.

Unlike my two previous tours on the islands, my family didn't accompany me this time. Judy and I didn't want to uproot the kids for what we thought would be a temporary assignment. It was hard to be away from my family for such a long period, but I traveled home every month and we talked frequently by phone.

During this second term, I had some problems with my chief deputy. As long as deputies do their job well, I don't care if they're male or female. In fact, as I mentioned earlier, when I was chief deputy, I hired the first female deputy to work in the islands. However, my female chief always seemed dressed in an inappropriate and unprofessional manner. She wore revealing outfits to the office, and I wasn't surprised to learn that she had a history of sexual harassment complaints. I addressed this situation by reinforcing that we were representatives of the U.S. Marshals Service and making it clear that I expected her attire and her behavior to be appropriate to her position. Once I made the rules clear, she straightened out.

Every trip that I made to paradise was worthwhile. Even though I loved the weather, which seems to be eighty-seven degrees year round, that wasn't the biggest payoff. What I loved most was the many friends I made, people I still speak with regularly. Some of them made special trips to the States to visit me when I was sick. We've become friends for life. It's not surprising to pick up the phone and hear, "Hey, Louie, how're you doing? When are you coming down?" Paradise has provided me with many lifelong friends; a man couldn't ask for better friends. It's these people who make sure that my time—both on the islands and off—continues to be paradise.

10
Interpol

Helping to Police the World

I f there's one law-enforcement agency with a lower public profile than the Marshals Service, it's Interpol. The agency's name is actually an abbreviation for the International Criminal Police Organization. Until someone brought the name up in conversation, I'd always thought Interpol was fictional, something that was invented for a James Bond film. I was surprised to hear that it was real. Some people still think this way about the Marshals Service, assuming that if we existed at all, we disappeared with the Wild West.

Interpol has never managed to get ahead of its low profile. During the three years I worked with the organization, I periodically staffed information booths with other Interpol representatives at law-enforcement conferences. We set up tables at annual gatherings of the National Organization of Black Law Enforcement Executives (NOBLE) and the International Association of Chiefs of Police (IACP) to help these police organizations understand our role and how we might help them. Many times people in the law-enforcement community approached us saying, "Oh, Interpol! You guys really do exist."

Formed in 1923 in Austria, Interpol is similar to the United Nations, except that it's entirely focused on law enforcement and international police cooperation. Each of the 187 member countries has a national central bureau, which is manned by its own law-enforcement specialists from various agencies. The country's local bureau is the single point of communication between that nation's police agencies and those of other member countries. This international communication helps to solve and prevent crimes. As member countries share information about drug trafficking, organized crime, fugitive apprehension, missing children, and counterfeiting, Interpol analyzes the information to detect trends in international criminal activity and shut down illegal operations.

Many countries stayed away from Interpol because it had fallen under Nazi control during World War II. After the European Allies from Belgium, France, the United Kingdom, and Scandinavia revived the organization after the war, Interpol's headquarters moved from Berlin, Germany, to Saint-Cloud, France, and the operation continued expanding. In 1989 its headquarters moved again, this time to the current location in Lyon, France.

The first suggestion that I should work for Interpol came during a conversation with Howard Safir, who was heading up some important operations for the Marshals Service. It was 1981, and I had just returned to the States after serving as chief deputy in the Virgin Islands. Howard had been talking with Dick Steiner, who was then the chief of Interpol's U.S. operations, known as the National Central Bureau. Interpol needed someone in the United States to take responsibility for fugitive apprehension. Since the attorney general had given the Marshals Service responsibility for the nation's fugitive cases in 1979, Howard was looking for someone to join Interpol and coordinate the international aspect of this operation. Whoever took the job would be the first person from the Marshals Service to work full-time within Interpol.

Interpol's members often need to determine if someone wanted by a foreign country is hiding in the States. At the time, the United States needed someone who could work with foreign investigators to find criminals we suspected were hiding in another land. Since the police from one country have no authority outside that country's borders, Interpol members offer each other necessary contacts and assistance. It was natural for Interpol to want someone from the Marshals Service to coordinate investigations from the U.S. bureau, which is located in D.C. and operated by the Justice Department.

As we talked, Howard related that he was looking for someone in the Marshals Service to act as a liaison with police counterparts from other nations, someone who knew about extradition and fugitive hunting. Because of the language barriers, this person needed good communications skills and the ability to get along well with a variety of people. Howard must have realized that I was already familiar with extradition, and my work in the Virgin Islands had already given me plenty of experience in dealing with French, British, and Dutch counterparts. He simply looked at me and said, "Louie, I think you'd be ideal for the job."

Initially I wasn't interested. I'd just settled into my new role in Witness Protection, and while my frequent job shifts make it appear that I adapt easily, I battle internal struggles whenever I have to make major changes. Periodically Howard would bring up the Interpol position when I saw him at headquarters. "I like what I'm doing," I told him one day. "Why would I want to leave and go to another agency, especially one that I don't really know anything about?" As we kept talking, I asked more questions about Interpol. Slowly the idea of working closely with people from other countries began to grow on me.

"Try it for a while," Howard finally said. "If you don't like it, we can bring you back. You're still part of the Marshals Service."

That discussion convinced me to take the next step, which was applying for the position. When the opening was announced within the Marshals Service, I put in my application, which involved providing the requisite details about my relevant assignments and experience. Within the fifteen-level civil-service pay grade, the position was rated as a GS-14, making it a high-ranking promotional opportunity.

After a while, John Toomey, the deputy director of the Marshals Service, contacted me. "Louie," he said, "everyone I've asked about you has nothing but good things to say. Once word got out that you'd put in for this job, no one else even wanted to apply. Everyone thinks that you deserve it. You're our man with Interpol now. You got the job."

Hearing that report from our deputy director was more gratifying than the job or the promotion that accompanied it. Knowing that so many of the people I worked with had such respect for me was a great feeling.

The offices for Interpol's central bureau were housed in the Justice Department building. Because Interpol is a cooperative effort that involves many law-enforcement agencies within a country, there were agents from the FBI;

the Drug Enforcement Agency; the Secret Service; the Bureau of Alcohol, Tobacco, and Firearms; the Immigration and Naturalization Service; and even the Department of Agriculture. The agricultural agents focused on international cases involving the theft and sale of food stamps. Because the Secret Service is part of the Treasury Department, these agents worked primarily on counterfeiting investigations and credit card theft. The FBI agents worked on terrorism cases, the DEA people concentrated on drug trafficking, while the marshals tracked down fugitives. We also had a few Canadians and some officers loaned by state and local police departments, which enabled us to efficiently work on cases requiring knowledge of local processes. Since everyone retained badges from their own department, Interpol gave us ID cards to confirm our assignments with them and provide access to various offices within the Department of Justice.

As the first person from the Marshals Service ever permanently assigned to Interpol, I knew that I'd be coordinating plenty of fugitive investigations. Still I was completely unprepared for just how much work was ahead of me. Many countries needed our help in apprehending fugitives they suspected to be hiding within our borders. When I arrived at my new office, I could barely see my desktop because of the stacks of folders providing information about this backlog of cases. The Marshals Service wisely sent me administrative help to wade through the heavy caseload that threatened to overwhelm me.

Every case within Interpol is classified by a color code. This system quickly helped me to understand and sort the many requests that came in. I learned that red notices were high-priority requests for us to assist with the apprehension, arrest, and extradition of wanted individuals. Blue notices were requests for information on criminal matters. In addition to fugitives, the Marshals Service also investigated missing persons, whose cases came as yellow notices. There were green notices that provided intelligence about potential criminal activity and other notices that either requested information or provided alerts to the global law-enforcement community.

My role was to act as a conduit, facilitating communication between the Marshals Service and law-enforcement agencies in other nations. Once I received a request for a fugitive investigation, I began gathering the necessary information for locating the criminal, using the same investigative process that I used when I worked in the warrant squad. I'd obtain the person's last known address; talk to family and friends; find out where he was last seen, where he might be headed; and obtain passport data and other identifying information. Then I funneled the information to Chuck Kuffer in the Marshals' Enforcement Operations Division, which specialized in solving fugitive cases. It always amazed me how quickly our deputies located these wanted criminals. When our own fugitive hunters apprehended someone, they would advise me and I'd begin communicating with the requesting country to start the extradition process.

Helpful procedures were in place to assist me when I had to communicate with my counterparts in other countries. Each of the Interpol offices used a codebook to facilitate the sending and receiving of information. It didn't matter if I had to send something to someone who spoke only Arabic or Russian; the coded messages we used enabled everyone to understand the communiqués in their own language. I became adept at quickly decoding incoming requests and informational messages.

The international nature of my role provided many wonderful travel opportunities. I remember spending two weeks in Ottawa working with the Royal Canadian Mounted Police, going to Belize and Santo Domingo, and traveling to other places I never would have visited. I even had the opportunity to return to the Virgin Islands when Interpol was conducting a big operation in the area. These trips typically centered on specific fugitive investigations that the United States and my host country were working on together. We followed up on recently uncovered details, shared any new information, worked on apprehending the criminals, and then began the extradition process.

The annual Interpol conferences gave me opportunities to meet interesting people and experience life in whatever foreign city was hosting that year's event, while enabling me to travel to Budapest, Hungary, and Berlin, Germany. It always amazed me whenever I gathered in a hotel conference room with my peers from other countries. Here I was, a country boy from rural South Carolina sitting with representatives from Russia, Germany, Africa, and Switzerland, listening to international speakers being translated into Interpol's four major languages: English, Spanish, French, and Arabic. At the sessions I attended, we learned more about efforts to curtail international criminal activity, how to foster better communication between our respective agencies, had many chances to exchange ideas, and heard about new methods to speed up the extradition of criminals.

At the conference in Cannes, France, in 1982, my hotel room was next to that of Manuel Noriega, who was then Interpol's delegate from Panama. I saw Noriega daily during this weeklong conference and even walked with him to sessions and sat next to him for dinner and cocktails. I admired his communication skills. A talk that he gave during one session revealed how well informed he was on a variety of topics and also demonstrated that he knew how to present himself effectively. He was short, had a pockmarked face, and typically wore a suit, not the military uniform that he frequently had on in later photos. He was pleasant company, was witty, and had a good sense of humor. I also discovered that we were both history buffs, which lead to many enjoyable conversations about this common interest.

Noriega also enjoyed talking about his country. He was hoping to get U.S. funding to provide assistance to the many poor people living in Panama. He thought it was great that our countries had such a healthy connection and appreciated the cooperative efforts that Interpol fostered. We both agreed that it was important to be able to call upon our peers in other countries for assistance. After the conference, we spoke a few times by phone about Interpol-related business. During these conversations, he was always pleasant and friendly. But I never saw him at another Interpol gathering.

I wasn't aware that he was doing anything illegal. Sometime after the conference, the DEA provided us with information about his drug-trafficking activities. After the U.S. military went into Panama to seize Noriega, the Marshals Service was asked to return him to Miami so that he could stand trial on a federal indictment for drug smuggling. While I was put in charge of this operation, I decided not to venture into Panama, letting my deputies handle the details so that Noriega and I didn't see each other. Currently he's still in prison, pending extradition requests from two countries.

Unlike United Nations gatherings, in which each country's participation is limited to one representative, Interpol's conferences are open to heads of participating law-enforcement agencies of the member nations. Even after my full-time involvement with Interpol ended in 1985, I was able to attend the conference held in Rhodes, Greece, in 2000, in my capacity as the Marshals' deputy director. My wife and children accompanied me to the conference that year, and they were able to see the sights and attend the social gatherings. They came into the enormous hotel conference room before the morning session started to get a glimpse of the three or four hundred people wearing nametags that identified what country they represented. At the time, I was seated up front with my counterparts from the DEA, FBI, and Secret Service. My daughter was very impressed. As they left the room before the session began, she told my wife, "I didn't know my dad was such an important person."

For my family, the best was yet to come. British actor Roger Moore was attending the conference, using his celebrity status as James Bond to draw attention to the plight of missing and exploited children, an important area of focus for Interpol. As it turns out, Moore had seen many Westerns and was a huge fan of the U.S. marshals. I spent a lot of time talking with him about his James Bond roles and answering his questions about the Marshals Service. He even joined my family for dinner, and we had our pictures taken together. My kids couldn't believe that they were having dinner with James Bond. And I couldn't believe that he was so happy about having his picture taken with a U.S. marshal. Additionally, the more that I worked with people in other countries, the more I witnessed their respect for the Marshals Service. Everywhere I went, it seemed that people wanted to talk with a marshal. Even my contacts in the legendary Scotland Yard loved the marshals. It always seemed odd that people outside the United States knew so much about our agency. Maybe they watched a lot of old Westerns or heard news reports about our work with the Witness Protection Program.

Tight security was standard procedure for the Interpol conferences because of the number of high-level law-enforcement officials gathered in one place. At the conference in Rhodes, Greece, armed guards with M-16s seemed to be everywhere. They kept watch in front of the hotel, patrolled in the corridors, and surrounded the buses we used for transportation. They even accompanied the spouses of attendees when they shopped.

While the security helped everyone to feel safe, it did make me a little paranoid and likely contributed to some of my superstitious behavior. We had tour buses equipped with translators for each of Interpol's major languages. For some reason, I was uncomfortable about getting on the English-speaking bus. Maybe I thought that Americans would be the primary targets of would-be saboteurs. Even though I didn't speak the other languages, I always rode the Arabic or Spanish bus. My kids didn't seem bothered by the security. They were impressed by the gun-toting guards, by the gunboats that escorted us to dinner on a Greek island, and by the exciting notion that their dad might actually be in danger.

The work with Interpol wasn't only about traveling to exotic places. We worked on a large number of important cases, including locating the CIA defector Frank Turple. Finding foreign fugitives hiding in the United States also boosted the marshals' reputation as fugitive hunters. I was proud to play such an integral role in helping other countries to lock up wanted criminals.

Because of my role with Interpol, I became quite friendly with people who worked in other agencies and expanded my knowledge of FBI, DEA, and Secret Service operations. Our working relationships also helped the agents to become more familiar with the Marshals Service and its duties. Sometimes this resulted in requests for assistance, which have continued throughout my career. For example, after the Oklahoma City bombing in 1995, the Marshals Service instituted policies to increase court safety. Only our deputies were permitted to carry guns inside federal courthouses. This policy created problems for the FBI's agents, and as a result, I received a call from the agent in charge in Seattle.

"Louie, I need you to do me a favor," he said. "Every time my guys go to the courthouse the marshals won't let them bring in their guns. They've got to leave them somewhere else, which is causing problems for us. Can you help me out?"

Allowing FBI agents to carry guns in federal courthouses seemed like a reasonable request, so I made some calls to our people in Seattle to solve this immediate problem. We also began instituting an exception to the firearms policy in other federal courts for FBI agents. This high-ranking agent wrote me a glowing letter of appreciation and called me to express his gratitude. I was able to fix a problem that had been frustrating the FBI simply because someone knew about the Marshals' role in the courts, remembered me from Interpol, and reached out.

Interagency cooperation was a daily occurrence within Interpol, as all of us reported to the deputy attorney general in the Department of Justice. Because our offices were so close together, we could walk down the hall and talk to our FBI or DEA counterparts and work out any problems. Communication between various agencies—even those with a history of rivalry—always seemed to go amazingly well. By giving us common goals and establishing an environment where cooperation thrived, Interpol really brought out the best in everyone.

The Marshals Service worked with Interpol to coordinate the first international fugitive operation. Working with agencies in England, Mexico, and Canada, we created the International Affairs Fugitive Task Force and developed a plan to apprehend a large number of fugitives wanted by these countries. We developed international warrants, something that no one had tried before, by getting assistance from the other Interpol task force members. Then each country's law-enforcement agencies executed the warrants, which enabled us to apprehend fugitives outside our own borders, where we lacked jurisdiction. This successful operation resulted in the arrest of more than two hundred fugitives within eight weeks.

My exposure to Interpol was extremely beneficial in many ways. Every new case provided opportunities to talk with people around the world who didn't always know much about the Marshals Service. And every time we successfully captured a fugitive and got publicity, it enhanced our reputation within the Department of Justice. It gave me enormous experience in learning to balance the needs of various officials, which became useful as my career advanced. On a daily basis we saw and answered directly to the chief of the U.S. piece of Interpol's operation, Dick Steiner, who had come from the Secret Service. However, I also had responsibilities that the Marshals Service expected me to fulfill. On top of that, everyone had to satisfy the attorney general, as our country's central bureau answered to the Justice Department. At times balancing what seemed like conflicting demands was difficult. The occasional turf wars with other agencies further complicated things. When turf wars arose, we would all sit down and work things out. Despite our somewhat different backgrounds, working together in Interpol helped us to overcome most issues. We didn't have many major disagreements, but when we encountered problems, we would sit together and talk until they were resolved.

Being in Interpol also provided some personal benefits. It was always helpful to know people when I traveled overseas, whether on business or for a vacation. I got advice on good hotels and tips on what to see. Sometimes my Interpol contacts helped me buy concert tickets or make restaurant reservations. When they traveled in the United States, I would return the favors. I still find it helpful to know that I can always pick up the phone and call an Interpol counterpart, regardless of the type of question I have. The level of cooperation we had was outstanding.

I learned much about how law-enforcement agencies operate in other countries, as well as how other people live. I gained a greater appreciation for my own country when I found out how few nations consider someone innocent until they stand trial and that often suspects are given no opportunity to post bail. Once a person is arrested, he or she remains in jail until the trial is completed. Talking about our investigative techniques was always enjoyable. I was often surprised to discover how many people around the world speak at least some English. And I was frequently a bit embarrassed at my own inability to converse in other languages.

I was quite gratified to be the first African American to work within Interpol in a law-enforcement capacity. Today several African Americans are assigned to Interpol by Customs, DEA, the State Department, and other law-enforcement agencies. As far as I know, I'm the only person who can claim to be the first.

My role with Interpol greatly expanded my experience in fugitive investigations. I learned much from my frequent interactions with the Marshals'

Enforcement Operations Division, as this division was responsible for investigating and apprehending the fugitives that came from our Interpol contacts. Finding wanted criminals is Enforcement's specialty and the division's deputies developed a great worldwide reputation as tireless manhunters. I must have learned the ropes fairly well because after three years in Interpol, the service promoted me to chief of enforcement. This meant that I had to leave Interpol, but it provided me with another promotion and an opportunity to run all fugitive investigations for the Marshals. I'm sure that my Interpol experience, as well as the people skills that I'd honed through my regular interactions with FBI and DEA agents, helped me to qualify for this position.

Working with Interpol was a rich and rewarding experience. I'm not suggesting that it made me wealthy. It really was worth more than all the money in the world. The education that I received from traveling, working with my counterparts in other law-enforcement agencies, meeting people who lived in other lands, and being exposed to other ways of doing things was priceless. I'll always be thankful for the opportunity to represent my country and to serve the Marshals Service within Interpol.

11
Top Cop

Running the Marshals' Fugitive
Apprehension Operation

I was nervous. It wasn't because of the top hat and cane that provided the finishing touches to the tuxedo I was wearing. It wasn't because I was the emcee standing before a roomful of more than one hundred people in the Washington Convention Center. It wasn't because of the many pairs of eyes focused on me. It was because the cue that I'd just given to my supporting team had been ignored and I didn't know what to do next.

On that December morning in 1981, everybody sitting before me in the convention center ballroom was excited. My audience had just feasted on a free breakfast and was waiting to hear the details about the free tickets they'd been promised to the upcoming Redskins-Bengals game. Most of them were hoping to win the grand prize: an all-expense-paid trip to Superbowl XX, a game that would soon be played in New Orleans. Smiling Redskins cheerleaders welcomed them into the room. People dressed in costumes used by team mascots—including an Indian and the popular San Diego Chicken character—were walking through the crowd, shaking hands and greeting everyone.

However, not everything was as it appeared that day. Both costumed characters were armed marshals, with their service revolvers hidden from sight. The cheerleaders were deputy marshals and D.C. police officers. My expectant audience was a Who's Who of the area's wanted posters, including bank robbers, drug dealers, and killers. Every one of them was a felon, some of them charged on multiple federal warrants.

We lured them to the convention center that day with official-looking letters from a company called Flagship International Sports TV. The company's initials—FIST—represented the code name for the service's Fugitive Investigative Strike Team. While I was posing as Flagship's CEO that day in my role as emcee, I was really the newly appointed chief of the Enforcement Operations Division, the team that I'd worked with to apprehend fugitives in my position with Interpol.

The FIST operations were launched in the 1980s as a creative way of dealing with a backlog of federal fugitive warrants. Three smaller sting operations had preceded this particular one, which was known as FIST IV. Together with my deputy chief, Bob Leschorn, I had worked for months to map out the complex operational and logistical plans. Bob was a natural choice to strategize our operation, as he'd been involved in similar efforts that deputies had carried out in the New York region. Under Bob's direction, deputies made fictitious calls to wanted men, pretending they represented an organization that had a gift for them. When the fugitives arrived at the address they were given, the deputies arrested them.

While we knew that FIST IV could produce a much larger number of arrests, both of us also realized that the stakes were much higher. In many respects, this operation was putting the Marshals' reputation on the line. Just a few years earlier, fugitive apprehensions were the FBI's responsibility. The attorney general had reassigned this work to the Marshals Service in 1979 to enable more specialization by each agency. We knew that the Justice Department, the FBI, and our own brass were watching, waiting to see whether the Marshals Service could shoulder this new role successfully. We couldn't afford any slipups.

From the day that the Marshals' associate director of operations, Howard Safir, called us into his office for the initial discussion, we had worked hard to pull this particular sting together. The idea, which had come from local marshal Herb Rutherford and his chief deputy, Toby Rooche, was to leverage smaller operations and work closely with local police departments to launch a cooperative fugitive program. While there had been smaller, similar operations in other states, it was clear that Howard, a no-nonsense manager, was expecting many high-profile arrests from FIST IV.

Bob and I held daily briefings to develop our plan and iron out any wrinkles. We obtained the last known addresses of Washington-area felons and mailed out more than three thousand letters. We worked out security plans with the convention center and received the needed support from the Metro Police, my old department. Then we staffed the operation with deputies and officers posing as ushers, porters, greeters, and cheerleaders. Somehow we even managed to convince Deputy Thomas Spillane to wear the San Diego Chicken costume.

As our guests arrived, Toby welcomed them at the door and checked their names off the list. We found clever ways to have our friendly greeters check these folks for weapons and disarmed quite a few of them. A hug from a cheerleader or an arm around a felon were both means of discreet weapons checks. Once we cleared the guests, Bob escorted groups of about thirty people into the ballroom, giving us additional time to monitor them, to see if we might need to keep an eye on a particularly unruly felon. As each group entered the room, we offered them coffee and doughnuts. When everyone was assembled and fed, it was time for my speech.

As the CEO of the company sponsoring the event, I stood in front of the room and got things rolling. Knowing that many in this crowd were likely Redskins fans, I talked about the exciting upcoming game and interacted with them. We had a prearranged signal with the Special Operations Group, which was supposed to enter the room when it heard me say "surprise." To my surprise, nothing had happened after I'd given the signal.

Thinking that I should repeat the cue louder, I decided to try again. "Today really is your lucky day," I shouted above the conversations. "And I've got a big *surprise* for you!"

This time the cue worked. With guns drawn, the SOG team swept into the room and surrounded the audience. The cheerleaders drew their weapons, as did the chicken and the Indian characters. Shock, anger, and surprise replaced the smiles and excitement on the faces in the room, as each wanted fugitive in the audience realized he or she was being arrested.

Surprise. My cue to the SOG team described many of the comments we heard as we handcuffed more than 120 wanted persons in what's been described by the major news networks, the Justice Department, and the local

police as one of the most successful fugitive operations ever. Many we arrested didn't realize the seriousness of the situation until they were handcuffed;
they actually believed the whole operation was an elaborate joke. Even then,
many handcuffed felons were disappointed to learn that they would not get
Redskins tickets when they were released from jail. As we transported them
to local lockups, one man commented that if he'd known we wanted him that
badly, he would have turned himself in. He thought it was miraculous that
no one had been hurt. There were a few muttered threats of lawsuits for false
advertising. A civil rights group accused us of unfairly targeting minorities,
but nothing ever came of it.

As the man in charge of the Marshals' fugitive apprehension operation,
I was pleased. This inexpensive sting went off without a hitch, and no one
was injured. The Washington, D.C., police reported a noticeable drop in area
crimes, and the scheme made headlines around the globe. We received calls
from police departments in other countries—Italy, France, Germany, Spain,
and Korea—that were interested in establishing their own sting operations.
At one point, I was even interviewed on a Korean news program. Years later
I saw our operation mimicked on TV shows and even in the movie *The Longest Yard*.

Once I approached my fiftieth birthday, I wasn't giving much thought to
advancing to another position. As much as I loved the Marshals Service, I
had built up enough service time to begin thinking about retiring. A visit to
headquarters to help with fugitive investigations, together with my regular
lunchtime run, changed that.

During my jog near our headquarters in McLean, Virginia, I bumped into
the service's director, Stan Morris. Because Chuck Kuffer had moved on from
his role as Enforcement chief, I was assisting the division with some operations. As we ran together, Stan asked me about my future plans. I mentioned
my thoughts about retirement, and he asked if I liked what I was doing in
Enforcement. When I said that I did, he asked if I'd like to continue doing it.
"Sure," I said, "but that job is probably already going to someone else." We
continued running, and neither of us said anything more about it. The next

day I was told that if I wanted to run the Enforcement Operations Division, the job was mine. Until I applied for the position through the proper channels, I would be the division's acting chief. Once again, no one else applied for the job and I was a shoo-in.

In some respects, working in Enforcement was like going home. The work was similar to what I'd done during my days on the warrant squad, except that the division apprehended fugitives for each of the ninety-four districts within the United States, as well as some who were wanted internationally. The fugitive investigation work that had been done separately by each district's warrant squad had been expanded into a national effort, which enabled a more integrated approach to the task. Nationalizing fugitive investigations also enabled us to create a career path for deputies interested in specializing in this work.

The deputies working in the nationalized Enforcement Operations Division focused solely on investigating federal warrants. Because they reported to us rather than to the local marshal, they didn't have to escort prisoners to trials, deliver subpoenas, or handle other court-related duties. Having fugitive investigators in each district office who weren't forced to spend time on the district's other work added considerably to our success.

Apprehending fugitives meant restoring order to our streets, as many felons became repeat offenders. When the attorney general gave the Marshals Service responsibility for pursuing fugitives in 1979, our jurisdiction expanded to include escaped federal convicts, bail jumpers, as well as probation and parole violators. When FBI agents developed a case, their agents retained responsibility for finding certain felons—bank robbers, kidnappers, and high-profile offenders who crossed state lines to evade prosecution. The Marshals Service had jurisdiction for all other federal offenses, from military deserters and those who defaulted on federal student loans to those who ignored speeding tickets on federal property. We also pursued felons whom other federal agencies—such as DEA and ATF—couldn't find.

The Canadian Mounties aren't the only ones who always get their man. In one year the Marshals Service makes more arrests than all other federal agencies combined. Among national and international agencies, we earned a well-deserved reputation as tireless fugitive hunters who followed hard-to-discern trails until the case was closed.

It doesn't matter how long an investigation takes; the Marshals Service doesn't quit. For twenty years we pursued one wily fugitive who had gotten the drop on federal agents and then kidnapped them. He intended to hold the agents for ransom, but they managed to slip out of their bonds and escape. The other agency couldn't find him, so it asked us to take the case. When we finally caught up with him, after years of intensive investigating, he was an old man living in Belize. He was shocked when our deputies showed up, and he begged them to let him go. "Please, please don't take me," he said. "I'm almost dead. Let me live the last few years of my life in peace."

The marshals' reputation as fugitive hunters is common knowledge among criminals. "Don't ever get those U.S. marshals after you," I've heard them say. "They never give up. They're going to catch you sooner or later." I saw more evidence of our reputation in a story in the *Washington Post* while I worked on this book. The article told how the service's investigators arrested another man they'd been pursuing for forty years. He was eighty-one years old when he was finally caught. In these cases, it's not our job to be the judge and jury. We can't let our feelings about a particular situation or the age of a fugitive enter into the case. We have to focus only on enabling the court system to do its work by finding fugitives and ensuring that they go to trial. By doing this, we safeguard the country's system of justice.

Eventually the Enforcement Operations Division's name was changed to Investigative Operations, which more accurately represents the work of following complicated trails until a felon is located. We check credit card, phone, and bank records, talk to neighbors, family members, and anyone else who might provide helpful information. We leave no stone unturned. The investigators in the division became so well regarded as fugitive hunters that they are all known by the nickname "Top Cop."

The Enforcement Operations Division's caseload was enormous. It even dwarfed the pile of warrants that nearly buried my desk when I first arrived at Interpol. As chief of the division, I had to sign off on every investigation in all ninety-four districts. While I was proud of the many cases we cleared each year, there were always hundreds of new ones waiting to be assigned to our investigators.

Dealing with the responsibility of finding these people was a nonstop job. Having a personal life became nearly impossible at times, as calls about escaped prisoners kept my home phone ringing on weekends and evenings. I'd often be awakened in the middle of the night when we were working on critical cases that involved a task force. It seemed like I never had any time off. Life became particularly rough when we were involved in the Con-Doc investigation, which focused on finding Terry Conner and Joseph Dougherty. Not only had these men escaped from prison, they were serial bank robbers who committed murders in Oklahoma, Indiana, Illinois, and Michigan. There was a lot of pressure on us to find them.

Monitoring and prioritizing the many cases we received was a constant struggle. We looked for ways to make sure that most violent crimes were quickly and effectively solved, while also ensuring that other cases were given the attention they deserved. Bob Leschorn developed a great idea for prioritizing these cases. To differentiate it from the FBI's Ten Most Wanted list, we called our list the Fifteen Most Wanted and used it to elevate the most heinous and violent fugitive cases to the national level. Having the list also enabled us to draw both public and media attention by highlighting our efforts to apprehend the most notorious offenders. The Fifteen Most Wanted list took off like an express train. As fugitives were arrested, we'd add another one to the list. I was particularly happy when we removed Conner and Dougherty from it in December 1984. We arrested these extremely dangerous felons in Black Forest, Colorado, after they'd been on the Fifteen Most Wanted list for a year and a half.

Initially the FBI wasn't very happy about our list, probably because the bureau saw it as in competition with its Ten Most Wanted list. In our minds, there was no competition, as the attorney general had clarified our separate responsibilities. The FBI's list resulted from cases that their agents were developing, whether they were white-collar criminals or money-laundering mobsters that they suspected of various crimes. When it came to our list, a federal case had already been made. When felons escaped from prison or jumped bail, they were considered fugitives and we had to find them. It was more cut and dried. (The FBI now maintains two lists. In addition to the Ten Most Wanted list that they've had since 1950, they created a Most Wanted Terrorist list after the September 11 attacks.)

Frequently there was rivalry between our agencies. For example, the FBI developed the case against the mobster Alphonse "Allie Boy" Persico but couldn't locate him when he failed to appear for sentencing. Our deputies went after him and apprehended him in a matter of months. It ruffled some feathers and bruised some egos at the bureau. Over the years I noticed that FBI agents often expected that they could come to our offices and see our files but didn't want to share their information. I put a stop to that, ensuring that we worked together more cooperatively. I established monthly meetings that enabled both agencies to function more like a team.

While it's not widely known, the FBI depended on the Marshals Service to make its arrests until the bureau was granted its own arrest powers in the 1930s. For many years FBI agents were strictly investigators; they didn't even carry guns until Congress gave them the authority to protect themselves from gangsters, like John Dillinger, whom they were investigating.

Bureau agents, however, still vastly outnumber U.S. marshals. The FBI has more agents in New York than we have in the entire service. If the bureau is looking for someone, it assigns roughly fifty agents to the case and supports them with four or five helicopters. The Marshals Service will have only two or three deputies looking for one person. Comparing the two agencies is like trying to find a mouse on an elephant's back. Since we are pursuing similar goals using our different strengths, our teamwork has always made sense. I'm glad that more cooperation developed, and that FBI agents now regularly work with marshals on various cases and task forces. When I left the Marshals Service, I worked as an investigator for the bureau and always enjoyed the people, the work, and the environment. I've been privileged to work in both of these stellar law-enforcement agencies.

During the five years I ran Enforcement, we executed approximately twenty thousand federal fugitive warrants every year. Some of these cases were fairly routine; others were complex investigations that pitted our staff of more than two thousand investigators against an array of street-smart criminals, spies, and just plain dangerous men.

One of Enforcement's first high-profile cases involved the hunt for Christopher Boyce, which was spearheaded by Howard Safir and became the basis for the 1985 movie *The Falcon and the Snowman*. Boyce had been convicted of espionage in 1977 when an FBI investigation revealed that he was selling U.S. satellite plans to the Russians. He had obtained the information using his top-secret clearance while working for a defense contractor.

After serving only a few years of his forty-year sentence, Boyce escaped from Lompoc Federal Prison in California. Something of a survivalist, he lived in the woods in California, Oregon, and Washington, supporting himself by robbing small banks during his nineteen months on the run.

We had regular jurisdictional disputes with the FBI over this investigation. Because Boyce was robbing banks, the bureau thought the case belonged to its agents. We argued that escapees from federal prisons belonged to us. The investigations remained separate.

We were initially worried because Boyce's father was a former FBI agent, and we weren't quite certain how to deal with this issue. The elder Boyce, however, made things easy for our investigators: he told them that he knew that we had a duty to perform. While I realized that he had to wash his hands of his son's situation, as a father, I felt for him.

Because Boyce escaped just three months after the attorney general changed the respective roles of the Marshals Service and the FBI in fugitive cases, this was our first high-profile fugitive case. The constant media speculation on Boyce's whereabouts made finding him and proving ourselves even more important. We received great support from Howard, my boss, who made sure that we had whatever we needed—from ongoing living expenses for our field agents to high-tech equipment.

Our investigators stayed on the case day and night. We organized task forces in various parts of the country when we got information that Boyce might be there. We checked his records, spoke to former girlfriends, and developed a profile based on the places and things that he liked. We knew he was an athletic guy and liked Etonic sneakers, so we regularly checked sporting goods stores to see if he'd been shopping. At various times during the investigation, we checked out tips that he'd been seen in Germany, Mexico, France, and Canada.

We finally captured him in a drive-in restaurant in Washington State. We'd gotten a tip that he was in the Seattle area, so we organized a task force to conduct surveillance. Our investigators spotted him sitting alone in his car, eating a sandwich. Once he was arrested, I received the call that the "falcon was in the cage" and was glad that we'd finally caught up with him. Boyce's capture did a lot to cement the service's reputation. The investigators who worked that case—including John Paschucci, Tony Perez, Sue Palmaro, and Danny Beherend—deserve a great deal of credit.

The Marshals Service's growing reputation led the Drug Enforcement Agency to ask for our help in finding the man responsible for the 1985 murder of one of its agents. Enrique "Kiki" Camarena was an undercover operative who infiltrated a Mexican drug cartel. When the cartel found out who he was, its members tortured him brutally for days before they finally murdered him.

The DEA wanted us to find the killers and bring them to justice. Since the agency's investigators suspected Rene Verdugo-Urquidez, a Mexican drug lord, we tried to persuade the Mexican government to cooperate. We even attempted to arrange extradition through the U.S. ambassador to Mexico, John Gavin, a tall, handsome former actor. When the Mexican government refused to work with us because they didn't want interference from American federal agents, we approached the Mexican police. We knew that the police had the ability to find him and tried to persuade them to help us with our case.

Just when we thought that Verdugo might be untouchable after all, the Mexican police contacted us. They had taken our fugitive across their border and left him in San Diego. We quickly drove to the location and found him— naked and bound to a tree—just as the Mexican authorities had promised. We took him to federal court in San Diego for arraignment. He was convicted of murder and received a long sentence.

The DEA organized an event a few years ago to honor Camarena. Everyone who worked on the case was there. It was like a family gathering, during which we remembered this fine agent's exemplary work, as well as the various aspects of the investigation. With Agent Camarena's family present, it seemed a fitting way for all of us to honor his memory.

In 1982 Enforcement's investigators also helped to capture Edwin Wilson, a CIA defector-turned-arms-dealer who reportedly sold munitions to Libya. Wilson had also been living in Libya. To entice him into the open, the deputies invited him to the Dominican Republic for a supposed arms deal. Luckily he took the bait. Then we arranged for Dominican Immigration to question Wilson's credentials and refuse him entry to the country. Because he was an American citizen with a U.S. passport, the immigration agents told him he had to get on the first plane bound for the States. When he boarded that New York–bound plane, he probably smelled a rat. Once he was back on American soil, the waiting deputies exercised their authority and promptly arrested him.

We also sent investigators to Honduras to arrest Juan Ramon Matta-Ballesteros, a big cocaine trafficker with connections to the cartels. There was an outstanding warrant for his arrest. Ballesteros was a modern-day Robin Hood. He used money from drug sales to help out the people near his home in the capital of Honduras, Tegucigalpa. It was difficult for us to find him because, just as in the Virgin Islands, none of the locals wanted to share information about one of their own.

Ballesteros was arrested when he went out alone for his regular morning jog. He physically fought our deputies, but they prevailed and extradited him to the States for trial. His arrest caused chaos in the Honduran capital, with rioters setting fire to an annex building connected with the U.S. embassy. We took a lot of heat on this arrest because Ballesteros was so well liked by the city's people. He was convicted on drug and murder charges and was sent to a maximum-security federal prison.

Bob Leschorn ran the Alphonse "Allie Boy" Persico investigation. Persico, who appeared on our initial Fifteen Most Wanted list, was responsible for extortion, dozens of murders, and other crimes. The brother of Carmine Persico of the Colombo crime family, he was an underboss in the Brooklyn branch of that syndicate and was wanted for failure to appear for sentencing. There was suspicion that he was hiding overseas, but we found him in

Connecticut. When we apprehended him, the media reported that "federal agents" arrested him, which made it seem like the bureau solved the case; it was just the opposite.

One of the cases that I found particularly intriguing, because of my interest in history, involved the search for Josef Mengele, a Nazi war criminal known as the Angel of Death. Mengele performed cruel medical experiments on people in Auschwitz. The Simon Wiesenthal Center, a Jewish human rights organization, was putting pressure on the Justice Department to either capture Mengele or prove that he was dead, since the Allies hadn't found him after the war. The Justice Department contacted the Marshals Service, and the case ended up in my division.

We created a task force and conducted investigations in Germany and in São Paulo, Brazil. During the investigation, we learned that Mengele had had a heart attack and drowned while swimming in São Paulo. After checking out this story, we identified his grave. The body was exhumed, forensic examiners identified it as Mengele, and the case was finally closed in 1985.

In addition to working with federal agencies, the Enforcement Operations Division frequently assisted state and local law-enforcement organizations. Sometimes we'd help out by conducting an investigation to locate an evasive fugitive. Sometimes we'd work together in a joint task force to execute state and federal warrants.

In Texas, for example, we found a fugitive wanted for a string of murders who was eluding the local law-enforcement community. Because our investigators found their targets in record time, we received many requests for assistance. As my deputy chief, Bob managed most of these investigations, freeing me to concentrate on getting the resources the division needed.

Before Bob or I arrived in Enforcement, smaller FIST operations were used primarily as federal efforts to reduce the backlog of existing warrants. We made it our goal to expand these unrelated efforts into a national program by working cooperatively with state and municipal law-enforcement agencies to give the operations another dimension. Neither of us ever dreamed that these creative FIST stings would become so successful.

After we netted more than 120 fugitives in the FIST operation at the Washington Convention Center, we organized a similar program in the Boston area. This time, instead of tickets to a football game, we sent felons invitations to win free tickets to a Boy George concert. Once again we arrested a large number of felons, cleared hundreds of outstanding warrants, and got dangerous criminals off the streets. And, once again, someone was upset with us. We heard that when Boy George returned to England after the concert tour, he filed a complaint with the State Department because we'd used his name without permission.

The success of these FIST stings led us to implement the program in metropolitan areas with large numbers of outstanding warrants. We even secured funding from the Justice Department to support these operations. Both state and local agencies jumped at the chance to work with us, as they often lacked the resources to pull off something of this scale. Typically, we'd organize a task force that consisted of our local investigators, deputies within the district, and local officers. In some cases, we even brought in DEA and ATF agents, when the operation required their expertise in drug deals, firearms, or explosives. We always kept our base of operations in the city we were targeting so that the agents were not distracted by their other responsibilities.

Planning these stings usually took six to eight weeks. We'd have to secure the warrants from the district federal court and then expunge the records, as sometimes people were caught and the associated warrants were never closed. Then we mailed the bait to the fugitives' last known addresses and waited to reel in our catch.

Each FIST operation revolved around a creative way to scam the fugitives to walk into our trap. In Tysons Corner, Virginia, our targets walked aboard a sleek black bus displaying the Playboy logo that promised to take them to an evening at one of the associated clubs. They walked right into the arms of female deputies—dressed as bunnies—and were promptly read their rights. In Miami, we enticed them with a chance to win a seven-day Caribbean vacation cruise. Our Dallas operation offered IRS rebate checks that somehow had not been claimed. In every case, the promised opportunity never materialized; all these felons ever saw was the inside of a jail and a courtroom.

Our management was extremely pleased at these highly successful operations, particularly because they were relatively inexpensive and resulted in no injuries to either our deputies or to the local law-enforcement officers. For some time, both Bob Leschorn and I were known as the "sting masters."

The Marshals Service has always had a touch-and-go relationship with the media. In many cases, we don't get credit for arrests, as reporters typically attribute our successes to "federal agents." Hollywood has sometimes helped us to break out of the frontier role most people still envision whenever the Marshals Service is mentioned.

Certainly TV shows like *The Fugitive* and movies like *U.S. Marshals* and *Con Air* have helped to raise the profile of the service. But the service's reputation has never gotten a better push than it received from John Walsh and his popular TV program *America's Most Wanted*. Our association with John has also been immensely rewarding on a personal level.

I came to know John in the aftermath of his son's kidnapping from a shopping mall in Hollywood, Florida, when the Marshals Service assisted in the investigation at the request of state officials. After Adam Walsh's heartbreaking 1981 murder, John decided to create an organization that would protect other kids, which eventually became the National Center for Missing and Exploited Children.

John went on to become the host of *America's Most Wanted*, using the program to profile unsolved crimes and encouraging the public to provide information to solve them. The Marshals Service worked closely with John on this show, providing many of the cases that were aired in his first programs and offering background about our work in fugitive investigations. Typically, after the episodes aired, we obtained tips that enabled us to solve the cases. Over time we established a good working relationship with John and the show and provided advisers to offer direction whenever our help was needed. While the FBI has also given advice for the show, the Marshals Service and John Walsh have always seemed to enjoy a special relationship.

I had the privilege of accompanying John to Capitol Hill for a breakfast meeting when he presented information to a committee focused on helping missing and exploited children. When his TV program decided to create a special feature for the service's bicentennial anniversary, I went to Tombstone, Arizona, to say a few words during the filming of the episode and got to watch the rest of the show that he was creating. John clearly loved the Marshals Service and was very enthusiastic about filming this special tribute.

John's TV show and his work protecting children led us to name him as the service's Man of the Year in 1988, an honor that isn't bestowed very frequently. In a ceremony filled with Justice Department officials, we thanked John publicly for helping to rid the streets of criminals and for assisting us in making the country safer. We separately named John as an honorary U.S. marshal in 2003, giving him a rare and distinguished position that is held only by a handful of people.

John is still a frequent speaker at the service's conferences and at special events. His example is a great role model for our country and his work in keeping the public informed about dangerous fugitives has done much to help the Enforcement Operations Division apprehend these people. I'm proud to call him my friend. He has proved that you don't have to carry a badge to be a Top Cop.

12
Working Retirement
Leading the Marshals Service

After five years of running the Enforcement Operations Division, I was approaching the service's mandatory retirement age of fifty-five. I could have stayed, but that would have meant submitting paperwork to get special approval from Congress. Since I didn't want to endure the red tape, I decided to officially retire.

My retirement party was reported to be the Marshals Service's biggest bash ever. At least, that's what many coworkers told me. Since retirement parties aren't typically recorded in the archives or the history books, I can't be 100 percent certain about that record. I do know that it was a very well-attended sendoff.

When I arrived at the Marriott Gateway in Crystal City, Virginia, on the day of the party, it was filled with people. There were local judges, DEA and FBI agents, coworkers from my Interpol days, and deputies and investigators from within the Marshals Service. The highlight of the celebration was entirely my son's doing. He was only eleven years old, but he stood up front to speak, unprompted by Judy or me. "You've all had my dad for a long time," he said. "Now it's time for him to come home to us." By the time he finished his brief speech, there wasn't a dry eye in the house.

Retirement is a funny thing. As I neared my fiftieth birthday, I began thinking about these leisure years more frequently and even started looking forward to the possibilities. I'd worked hard my entire life, starting with my childhood on the farm, and the idea of resting became appealing. When the time actually arrived, however, I became nervous and was second-guessing myself. Now, I'm the first one to admit that I've been an unsuccessful retiree. If someone graded me on how I've spent my leisure years, I'd definitely deserve an F. There's been no shuffleboard, no bingo, and very little fishing. Even though I "retired," I've never stopped working. I guess I have a hard time sitting still for very long.

Not long after my retirement from the Enforcement Operations Division, my friend Al Meyers, a retired FBI agent, told me that the bureau was looking for people to fill contract positions as background investigators. After Al's recommendation, I made a few follow-up calls and landed an interview with Marty Mulholland, the chief of the FBI's Background Investigation Contract Services (BICS) Unit. Because of my investigative background and Al's status as a highly regarded former agent, I was hired almost immediately, making me the first outsider that the agency ever hired to conduct these investigations. On the first day of the orientation training, I felt like the new kid in school. Everyone was asked to stand and provide a brief description of his or her background. All the others had been agents in charge of various districts or operations within the bureau. When my turn came, everyone began muttering because I came from a competing agency. I later learned that these background investigation jobs normally go to the bureau's retired agents. It was a great way to take care of the FBI's own people, something I understood.

Chief Mulholland quickly stopped the disapproving chatter. "He's here, and he's going to stay here," he told the class. "Now let's move on." After that I didn't have any problems from anyone. Conducting the investigations was enjoyable, and my work received some rewarding feedback. More than a few people told me that I should have worked with the bureau instead of the Marshals Service, as my reports couldn't be distinguished from their own agents' reports. Somehow, they said, I must have fallen through the cracks and ended up with the wrong agency. It was a great compliment. In between my appointments as marshal to the Virgin Islands in 1984 and 1993, I continued these background investigations and was even contracted by the State Department to handle this same work for the Diplomatic Security Service.

I was happily conducting investigations when the Marshals Service rang my phone again. This time the service informed me that I was being considered for the director's position. While I was honored, I didn't get my hopes up. This wasn't the first time that my hat was tossed into that ring. I'd also been considered after I returned from my second tour as marshal in the Virgin Islands in 1993. That appointment went to Eduardo Gonzalez, who hailed from Florida, the same state as Attorney General Janet Reno. The choice was understandable.

This time I learned that my good friend John Marshall was also being considered for the director's job. I'd known John for many years. Following his successful career as a state trooper in Virginia, John had been appointed as the U.S. marshal for Virginia's eastern district. During one of my visits to headquarters, back when I was working in the Virgin Islands, someone mentioned that a young man had just taken the helm in Virginia. Knowing that he was new to the service, I introduced myself and offered to help him become better acquainted with his role and the Marshals Service. I offered him the benefit of my years of experience, saying that I was always available if he needed advice. Over the years we established a solid friendship, one that enabled us to have a long talk about the director's vacancy. It took a while for us to agree on our respective roles because each of us wanted the other to have the top spot.

"Louie, you know more about the service than I do," John told me. "Why don't you take the director's chair and I'll be your deputy director? Everybody knows you. I'm an unknown; I'm not a career man like you. That would work out fine for both of us."

I considered it but disagreed. John was the son of Thurgood Marshall, the Supreme Court justice and civil rights pioneer. John's brother, who was named after their father, was serving as assistant to the president and cabinet secretary on President Clinton's staff. I thought that the service would benefit from having John as director.

"John, your brother works for the president, you've got a lot of clout there, and having the son of Thurgood Marshall would be good PR for the service. Why, you even have the right name for this position," I said jokingly. "What would be better than having a guy named Marshall as head of the Marshals?"

"No, Louie," John replied with a smile. "No one deserves this position more than you. I want you to have it."

We went back and forth like that for quite a while. Finally, I told John that I was leery of the pressure that accompanied the top position. I'd handled stressful situations before, but nothing of this magnitude. As director, I'd be responsible for the entire staff of the service—all six thousand people. I'd have to handle complaints from our people, as well as those coming from anyone else. And I'd also have to deal with the expectations of the White House, Congress, and the Justice Department. My concerns must have been convincing because once I finished explaining my issues, John agreed.

"OK, Louie, let's do it," John said. "I just want you to know that I still think that you should be the director, not me."

After we spoke, John received the nod for the job. The plan called for me to come in as his deputy director. We were later surprised to learn that someone had been lobbying the administration to have a different person named as John's deputy director. When I discovered this, I felt betrayed but soon realized that it was just politics. I didn't want to fight city hall and would have happily thrown in the towel. Instead, John approached Attorney General Reno to work out a compromise. They decided that Mike Ramone, a former deputy from Los Angeles who had come up through the ranks, would become deputy director, and I was named as John's special assistant.

When John was sworn in on February 1, 2000, after being confirmed by the Senate in November, it was an historic event. He became the first African American to serve as the director of the Marshals Service. Coincidentally, his swearing in fell on the first day of Black History Month. The Bible that John placed his hand on was the same one that his father had used in 1967, when he was sworn in as a Supreme Court Justice. It was even open to the same page. Although his father had passed away, John said that he could almost sense his presence during the ceremony. When John left college to pursue a career with the Virginia State Police, Thurgood didn't discourage him or lecture him on the importance of education. Instead, he encouraged his interest in police work by telling him stories about how the U.S. Marshals had enabled great strides in integration in the South. John's father was a big fan of the Marshals Service, which both influenced and encouraged John's law-enforcement career.

I spoke at the celebration following the ceremony at John's request, which meant that I had to stand up in front of Attorney General Reno, Justice John Paul Stevens and Justice David Souter, Deputy Attorney General Eric Holder, Senator Charles Robb, as well as other senators, the U.S. attorney for the D.C. area, and White House officials. I remember watching the Army/Navy Band, holding my three pages of notes, which seemed to weigh a ton, and wrestling with the fear of speaking in front of the press, as well as this roomful of prominent people. It scared me to death; I felt like a poor country boy again.

Once I began, my nervousness passed and everything was fine. I started out with jokes about John's nickname, since many people in the service either referred to him as "Marshal Marshall" or as "M squared." When I comment-ed that it must feel nice to have an entire agency named after you, everyone laughed, which helped me to loosen up.

"When I was serving as the marshal in the Virgin Islands," I continued, "John would call me frequently for advice. I guess whatever I said to him must have been pretty good. If it hadn't, I probably wouldn't be standing where I am today, speaking to all of you and eating this good food." I don't remember much else about my speech. I do recall that when I stepped down from the podium, I was surprised that everyone gave me a standing ovation.

The highlight of the evening, and the most touching part for me, was John's commentary on our friendship during his speech. "This man came to me out of the clear blue sky," he said. "He didn't want anything. He simply told me he'd be more than glad to help me, to steer me, and he has." John also clarified that I had stepped aside so that he could be the director. It was a great gesture on his part. I was pleased to help him and was honored that he would mention such a simple act in front of everyone. It made me even prouder of our friendship and excited about the work we would be doing together.

In addition to being the service's first African-American director, John also made history as the first former marshal to serve as director. As strange as that might sound, many of the service's directors came from state police organizations or departments in large metropolitan areas. For example, Eduardo Gonzalez came from the Miami police department and Wayne Colburn from San Diego's force. John's experience in leading one of the districts offered him a distinct advantage: he came to the job with an in-depth knowledge of the service's internal operations.

John had also been active in various leadership roles within the service that gave him a valuable perspective on our organization. He had served as head of our leadership council, a group that focused on helping our people to improve their leadership skills, and included chief deputies and marshals from other districts. He had also been an adviser to the director and was invited to attend many of the meetings of the director's senior staff.

The duties of deputy director were essentially split between Mike Ramone and me. Because of my relationship with John and the level of trust between us, in many respects, I functioned much like an aide for a military officer. All memos and communiqués came across my desk before they could be transmitted, enabling me to ensure that no changes were required. Some of the items that I worked on actually should have gone to the deputy director, but John often decided to send certain responsibilities my way.

The job had certain perks. On a couple of occasions, I accompanied John to the White House when his brother invited us. During one visit, we were all having dinner in the staff dining room. The door opened and in walked President Clinton. I was amazed when he walked right up to our table and greeted each of us. It was enough of a thrill just to be at the White House.

While John was in leadership, we focused on straightening out our budget process and hiring more deputies. In many respects, these two important initiatives were related. Without the necessary funds, we couldn't justify additional salaries, no matter how badly we needed the manpower. Here John's field experience proved essential. Instead of having headquarters take a top-down approach to budget planning, we turned the process on its head by asking the districts to tell us what their staff and resource needs were. Then we added our headquarters' requests to those numbers. We received terrific feedback from the field and then created an improved method that helped to validate our budget requests.

With the budget straightened out, we were able to begin hiring. In many areas of the country, we lacked the staff needed to perform all of our responsibilities adequately. Some districts even struggled with basic tasks: for example, they didn't have enough deputies to transport prisoners to court. Because of overcrowded jails, they had to house and transport prisoners from many different facilities, creating daily logistical problems. The budget process enabled us to create new positions to help solve such difficulties. We also created a communications command post that operated around the clock, something that was sorely needed in many field operations to relay command decisions from headquarters. And we were able to begin promoting some deserving people. Sylvester Jones, who provided leadership in the Enforcement Operations Division, was promoted to an assistant director's slot. The whole promotion system was an important area of focus for us. We wanted to make it faster and easier to fill empty positions once someone moved into a new role. We knew that it took too long to fill these vacancies so we implemented some new procedures to change this, including reducing the amount of paperwork required by applicants and expediting the promotion process. I chaired our Equal Employment Opportunity committee, which examined ways to encourage the service's workforce to more closely mirror the country's diverse population.

Our focus on filling positions didn't make us immune to personnel changes. After about a year, Mike Ramone decided to leave his role as deputy director. Suddenly, everyone wanted me to move into that role. Predictably, I wasn't eager to move anywhere, even though my duties would essentially be unchanged. It took a few conversations with John for me to decide to step into the official role as deputy director. I agreed simply because he needed my help. While I was hesitant to take on additional pressure, the new role meant I'd be able to enjoy more travel opportunities in order to attend conferences in which we participated.

As deputy director, my role was different from John's role in the same ways that a chief deputy's duties differ from the local marshal's. John's focus was primarily external. He attended meetings with the attorney general, the Justice Department, and the White House. As his deputy, I was to focus on the service's day-to-day operational needs. In many ways, my role was like that of a chief of staff. My understanding of John's objectives meant that I could make decisions on his behalf, but I still checked with him regularly to ensure that we were on the same page. And I continued reviewing various documents and memos, always letting him know what wasn't ready to be transmitted and what had to be corrected.

If John was traveling to a district, something that he liked to do, I ran interference for him. I enjoyed contacting the district as his advance man, asking about what was going on there before he arrived and ensuring that he was always fully informed and not blindsided by anything. I found out where he was supposed to be, assembled the schedule, and then briefed him. I always secretly enjoyed hearing and seeing how people reacted when they heard from the deputy director. It was always, "Oh yes, sir, Mr. McKinney." For a country boy like me, it was always a bit of a thrill.

As the year 2000 approached, we heard many warnings about the widespread computer problems that would occur when the clock rolled over in the new year. These concerns increased our vigilance in protecting the federal judiciary, as guarding them from any threat—human- or computer-related—remains one of the primary missions of the Marshals Service. We were more sensitive to anything that could be considered threatening, proactively offered additional training to court security personnel, and relied on a sophisticated threat-assessment program.

Anyone in government work will tell you that one of the toughest challenges is getting cooperation from other agencies. Taking a chapter from my time in the Virgin Islands, we decided to work on improving rapport with our counterparts at the FBI, DEA, and similar groups. Every month we held a meeting in which we came to a better understanding of each other and learned how we could improve our working relationships. Initially the Marshals Service sponsored these gatherings, chairing the meetings and bringing the food. As our relationships improved, the other agencies began sharing this responsibility. While scheduling a time that everyone could meet was always a challenge, we all witnessed the direct benefit of improved communication from these sessions.

◆ ◆ ◆

Since the director's position is a political appointment, when President Clinton's term ended, we knew that we would soon be making way for a new director appointed by the next president. On the day that George W. Bush was sworn in, we busily packed up our offices, as we had been politely informed that the director's office should be empty by 4:00 p.m.

It was a sad day. After helping John with his boxes, I went to my office and began taking pictures off the wall and packing up my things. Hearing a knock on the door, I looked up to see one of the people from the Bush administration's transition team. She was glancing around my office, but with a strange look on her face.

"Louie," she asked, "what are you doing?"

"I'm packing," I replied. "John's office is all finished up, and I'm just clearing out my stuff. I won't be long."

Stepping closer, she said, "No, Louie. You don't understand. We want you to stay on and run the Marshals Service."

She continued talking, but I was so shocked that I don't think I heard a single word she said. My loyalty to John made it difficult for me to even comprehend how she could make such a statement. For a few moments, I stood there looking at her. Then I shook my head and continued packing. "No way," I replied. "I couldn't do that to John. You ask him to leave and expect me to take his job? I could never do that."

The Bush administration, however, was persistent. I was between a rock and a hard place, as I felt that I was being forced to choose between friendship and a presidential request. Not knowing what else to do, I spoke to John about the offer and my feelings about the request. John listened for a while and then put the issue in perspective for me. "Louie, if you don't take this job, somebody else will," he said. "You could continue to carry out the policies and the work that we set in motion. Besides, you're simply the best man for the job."

The next day a courier delivered an official letter from the White House, signed by President Bush, making me the director of the Marshals Service. While the letter is still proudly displayed on my wall, I remember it as a bittersweet moment. I wished that John could have stayed. I was particularly upset because the change had put him out of work. When you're in an appointed position and the administration changes, you can take an open slot at the highest level you held prior to the appointment. Since John had previously been a U.S. marshal—another appointed position—he had nowhere to go. I was happy when he was named as Virginia's secretary of public safety, which gave him responsibility for the state police, the National Guard, and the Department of Corrections. The state of Virginia obviously knows what a good man they have in John. Even though former governor Mark Warner originally appointed John, when Governor Tim Kaine took office, he reappointed him. Our friendship is still strong; we remain in close contact and talk frequently.

For some time, my friends in other agencies had encouraged me to become director of the Marshals Service. Both Louis Freeh at the FBI and Donnie Marshall—no relation to John—at DEA thought I should go after the job. "You know a lot of people, you've been around for a long time, and you have a depth of experience in many different roles," Donnie told me. "You need to be the director." Climbing the ladder to the top isn't my style. Doing work that I enjoy has always been enough to satisfy me.

Even though I was running the Marshals Service, I technically wasn't the director; I was the *acting* director. Appointing a director is an involved process, requiring FBI background checks, reviews of pertinent experience, and then confirmation from the Senate Judiciary Committee. Because the president needed someone quickly, someone who was capable of running the service on a short-term basis, I was appointed in an acting capacity. I had all the authority that a director could exercise; I lacked only the Senate confirmation.

With an acting director in place, the administration bought time to search for a permanent replacement, which was strictly a political consideration. The White House believed that appointing an Hispanic director to the Marshals Service would satisfy an important bloc of voters for the next election. I learned that other officials in the administration had mixed feelings about looking for a permanent director. The new attorney general, John Ashcroft, told me, "Louie, everybody wants you in that job, including me. You're doing great things, and you deserve it. But the administration thinks that it can leverage the position and make it easier for the president to get reelected."

I've never been a political person. I was proud to serve the president and the service that had done so much for me. I had a job to do and never allowed political considerations to affect my attitude or get in the way of the important work we were doing.

Politics aside, having me in the director's office was an achievement for the Marshals Service, as I was the first career deputy to run the service. Because I'd started out as a deputy and spent more than twenty-five years working in nearly every major operation, I had a number of advantages over previous directors, who typically came from outside the service. There was little about serving the judiciary, transporting prisoners, protecting witnesses, apprehending fugitives, and seizing assets that I didn't know. Since I'd worked my way up through the ranks, I had virtually no learning curve and hit the ground running. Knowing the nuts and bolts of the operation also made it difficult to pull anything over on me. Whether it was budgets or operations that were being planned, I knew what had to be done and where to find the best people to do it. I had an intimate knowledge of what it took to conduct nearly every operation and could quickly detect and correct problems. For example, while I was reviewing one district's operation, I learned that someone had told the marshal that he wasn't entitled to a car and a driver for official business. I straightened that out and made sure that everyone knew that a marshal was permitted to have a car.

I also understood problems in a way that previous directors couldn't because of my background and experience with the service's culture. The Marshals Service has always been a close-knit operation that isn't particularly welcoming of outsiders, and this has put many a novice director at a disadvantage. I was able to operate on a completely different level. My tenure also earned me a degree of respect within the ranks. Because people knew where I came from, they often told me that they were confident that I'd understand their issues, as well as what it took to mount a successful operation. They knew that they could count on me for support, as well as for getting them what they needed to finish the job.

Even the attorney general's office began to realize the benefits of having a career man in the director's spot. One day the attorney general's chief of

staff asked me why other qualified people in the service never expressed interest in becoming director. I explained that everyone thought that the position
was reserved for outsiders, for people who were typically political appointees.
Within the service, most of us assumed that the highest position that we could
ever attain was chief. It never occurred to anyone that they would ever be considered for the director's spot. Since my pioneering effort, there's been good
progress in placing career people into that office. John Clark started out on
the ground floor as a deputy in San Francisco, capping his twenty-four-year
career with the Marshals Service by being confirmed as director in 2006.

One of my first important decisions as acting director was who to bring
in as my second in command. The decision was actually a fairly easy one. I'd
known Stacy Hylton for a number of years. She had already distinguished
herself in the service as the first woman to pass the strenuous training for
the Special Operations Group. I knew that she was a tenacious, hardworking
chief deputy in Columbia, South Carolina, and that she'd be equally effective
as deputy director. I was proud to help her to break the glass ceiling at the
Marshals Service by naming her as our first female deputy director.

My knack for getting along with people helped me to accomplish many
things while I served in the director's office. I always made it a practice to
talk to everyone I could, from the chiefs and marshals in the districts to copy-
machine operators, secretaries, and maintenance workers. It doesn't cost
anything to be nice to people, to treat them with respect, and it often results in
benefits for everybody. I was always willing to go to people with my hat in my
hand, both inside and outside the service, and to ask for what I needed. Because I approached them in a forthright fashion and laid things on the table, I
usually was able to secure what we needed to get the job done.

We focused primarily on continuing John's work in budget planning, hiring, and promoting people. With the budget process in place, justifying any
budget increases was much easier. As a result, we were able to fill many vacancies within districts that had been vacant for as long as five or six years. We
were also able to continue promoting many deserving people.

A large portion of the budget funds that we secured was earmarked for
building and improving federal courts. Because the federal courthouses must

be secure, the Marshals Service is intimately involved in planning these construction efforts. While lovely, old buildings housed many of our courts, some of these structures were difficult to equip with the necessary security features. For example, the court in the Old Town section of Alexandria had no safe port for unloading prisoners. As they were transported for trial, they stepped right off the bus and onto the sidewalk with everyone else. The new building that was erected not only had a secure place for prisoners, it had separate corridors for prisoners and judges, as well as the latest in high-tech equipment. We also planned for adequate office space for the marshals in many of these buildings, something that had never been accounted for before. There was much work involved in these court construction efforts, but we continued working diligently to accomplish this important goal.

Since no leadership position or organization exists in a vacuum, I faced a number of challenges both inside and outside the service. One of the biggest was dealing with the political environment. Someone once told me that the political considerations inside the beltway will eat you alive if you're not careful. To begin with, as the director, I was working for many different bosses and was under constant scrutiny. I regularly took calls from Capitol Hill, the White House, and the Justice Department. There were calls from other federal agencies, from state agencies, and from crime commissions. There was no shortage of problems fighting for my attention. If I dropped one of the many balls that I happened to be juggling, someone quickly noticed and sometimes created a ruckus over it. Since the marshals are general practitioners within the law-enforcement community, there were always requests for us to do various tasks. On top of our normal operations and special requests, I also had to deal with those who wrote their congressional representatives because their sons weren't hired or promoted quickly enough, despite the fact that they didn't meet our qualifications.

It seemed like I was constantly under the gun, and this affected my personal life. Very late one night, a prominent official called me at home. "Louie," he said, "you'd tell me if we lost a plane, wouldn't you?"

Shocked by his statement, I didn't know exactly how to respond. All I could muster up was, "Pardon me, sir?"

When he repeated his question, I told him that I'd certainly let him know if one of our prisoner transport planes had gotten into trouble. Promising to get back to him, I spent hours checking out this supposed hijacking and turned up absolutely nothing. Since all of our planes were accounted for, I called the official back so that he could follow up with the White House. To this day, I don't know what prompted this call. There were other times when I was roused from sleep and had to drag myself into the office because a prisoner escaped, there was a break in a major fugitive case, or we had a problem with our own deputies. It was a challenging, demanding role. There were many times when my family didn't see much of me.

There were also times when I encountered subtle racism from the many good ole boys inside the beltway. They didn't seem particularly pleased to be dealing with someone who wasn't white. They didn't come right out and openly communicate their displeasure, but it was clearly present in their body language, their statements, or both. After many years in government work, I'd learned to detect and deal with these encounters without allowing them to impede my work. I just moved on, refusing to let someone else's problems become my problems. Besides, I knew that John had experienced similar treatment.

Despite our regular sit-downs with other federal law-enforcement agencies, there were still frustrating moments when we were in each other's way, when another agency was unwilling to share information, or when we had to deal with ongoing turf wars over jurisdiction on a particular case. In these situations, I constantly emphasized that we were all either working for the same person—the attorney general—or that we shared the common goal of getting the bad guys off the streets. Those shared values were more important than who finished first. Whenever a situation became too intense, I reminded everyone about what mattered most. Even the people who might not like the Marshals Service or me couldn't disagree with that perspective.

There were also challenges outside the beltway. We had ninety-five U.S. marshals across the nation, each of them appointed by the president. In some cases, they didn't care what headquarters had to say. If headquarters didn't like what a marshal was doing and that marshal refused to make changes, there wasn't much we could do about it. The power of the appointment could typically keep that person in office, as he or she usually had a connection to a senator, a governor, or some other person in power. In the past, we had little leverage with which to dismiss marshals, unless they acted illegally. During my tenure, we were able to say good-bye to a few of these Lone Ranger types.

I'd been acting director for just over six months on the morning of September 11, 2001. I was driving to work when a staff member called to tell me about a possible movie stunt at the World Trade Center. By the time I arrived at our headquarters in Crystal City, Virginia, we knew it was an attack. Sitting in the office, watching the events unfold on TV, I heard a noise and turned to see a plane that looked like it was flying nearly upside down. At first I thought that the pilot might have missed the runway while trying to land. A few moments later the whole building began to shake and dust and soot flew from the vents. We were feeling the effects of the crash into the neighboring Pentagon.

People began scrambling to find safety, and we quickly began evacuating the building and locking it down. There was panic evident on people's faces, as we knew that any of the dozen planes that were still unaccounted for might be headed toward the Washington, D.C., area. We had just started moving our whole operation toward our command center when word came that I should head to a secure location along with others from the attorney general's office and the Justice Department. I declined, electing to stay with my people. It was days before I was able to head home again and see my family.

After we established communication with our deputies in New York, we began assessing our next steps. Along with a contingent of twenty-five deputies, I made the trip to Ground Zero to aid in the search-and-rescue operation. The sights and smells were horrific. It was a war zone, a sight worse than anything I'd seen in the aftermath of the Oklahoma City bombing, where I'd helped with investigations in my consulting role with the FBI. Both the Marshals Service and ATF agents arrived at the Trade Center site with dogs that were trained to find people. After a while, the dogs began to show their frustration at their inability to find anyone. To settle them down, some of our people had to hide and let the dogs find them.

When we returned to headquarters, I began working with the attorney general's office, responding to requests to send deputies to the airports. Still battling our own staff shortages, the Marshals Service lost the opportunity to reestablish the successful sky marshal program. However, we continued doing our part to enhance the heightened security at our nation's airports by guarding planes, securing our airport operations, and providing a presence to prevent further attacks.

My first direct contact with terrorism preceded the events of September 11. As an FBI consultant, I was sent to the site of the Oklahoma City bombing. Nothing I saw or heard on the news prepared me for the devastation that I witnessed. Somehow I managed to finish the investigative work that I was sent there to conduct.

While I served as acting director for the Marshals Service, we were involved in the execution order for Timothy McVeigh, the bomber convicted of the destruction of the federal building in Oklahoma City. Because he was a federal prisoner sentenced to death, the order for his execution had to go through the Marshals Service. After receiving the execution plans, I awaited the call from the Justice Department's command center. On June 11, 2001, I received the call to carry out the court-ordered execution. I immediately relayed the order to Frank Anderson, the marshal in Indiana responsible for communicating with the Bureau of Prisons team that administered the lethal injection.

As the Marshals' acting director, I regularly fulfilled a variety of public speaking tasks and ceremonial duties. Some could be routine, but they had important implications for the service. Others, like addressing school assemblies, were just plain fun. Without a doubt, one of my most intriguing duties was appointing an honorary U.S. marshal who became the very first "space marshal." When I flew to Johnson Space Center in 2001 to appoint NASA astronaut James Reilly as an honorary marshal, it took the Marshals Service far beyond our previous orbit as sky marshals.

Becoming an honorary marshal is a rare privilege. At the time, the service had appointed only six of these honorary positions during its entire history. The impressive list of honorary marshals included former president Ronald Reagan, comedian Bob Hope, and James Arness, the actor who played Marshal Matt Dillon in the long-running TV show *Gunsmoke*.

Each honorary marshal is selected based on his or her ability to raise public awareness for the service. James Reilly took his badge into space during two space shuttle missions, making these trips historic occasions for our two agencies, both of which captured the imaginations of many Americans. Jim became the first marshal to travel in space, but he won't be the last. One day there will probably be many more space marshals. For now, I am happy to have played a part in naming the first one.

Congressional testimony was another aspect of my role as acting director. I had to present the service's accomplishments, highlight our plans, and justify our budgetary requirements to the Judiciary Committee. Not long after my appointment, I also testified before a subcommittee investigating racial profiling in federal law enforcement agencies. I answered a variety of questions about our practices, as did Donnie Marshall; Tom Picard, the deputy director for the FBI; and Kathy Hawk-Sawyer from the Bureau of Prisons. The marshals emerged unscathed from the investigation, primarily because we pursued fugitives only when cases had already been made and were merely executing against the existing warrants.

While fulfilling a speaking obligation at Constitution Hall, I found myself glancing nervously at the other speakers sitting on the stage with me. There was a Supreme Court justice, the attorney general, the deputy attorney general, and the heads of the other law-enforcement agencies. None of them appeared to be sweating or shaking like I was. I have an intense fear of public speaking, one that nearly rivals my dread of snakes.

Each of us on the stage had been asked to provide an overview of our agency's work and recent accomplishments. I had a firm grasp of this information, but that didn't seem to help me much. Looking out into the audience, I knew there were many members of Congress present. In my nervous state, it looked to me like everyone else in the world had come too. I was so worried that I'd foul up that I wondered if everyone could hear my knees knocking and sense my jangling nerves.

During these kinds of engagements, it was almost as though I was present in two different forms. I was certainly standing behind the podium, reading my notes with a shaky hand, and wishing that my mouth wasn't so dry. Standing close by my official-looking self, though, was a barefoot country boy from South Carolina. He was smiling up at me, both surprised and pleased at our progress and our good fortune.

Index

Alias Program, The (Graham), 123

American Gangster, 114

American Indian Movement (AIM), 88, 89, 92–93, 96–98

America's Most Wanted, ix, 170

America's Star, 39

Angel of Death, 168

Asbury Park, New Jersey, 16–17, 50

Ashcroft, John, 182

ATF. *See* Bureau of Alcohol, Tobacco, and Firearms (ATF)

Barboza, Joe "the Animal," 109, 113, 126

Beall, Carlton, 31, 33, 36

Boyce, Christopher, 165–166

Bridges, Ruby, 36, 55

Brophy, John, 60, 55

Brown, H. Rap, 118

Brown, James, 13–14

Buffalo Soldiers, 95

Bureau of Alcohol, Tobacco, and Firearms (ATF), 5, 29, 136–137, 141, 161, 169, 187

Butler, Al, 31–32, 35–36, 51, 55

Calhoun, Frederick, 31, 33, 34, 55

Camarena, Enrique "Kiki," 166–167

Carter, Mel, 140

Clark, John, 184

Colburn, Wayne, 74, 178

Con Air, 46, 170

Con-Doc investigation, 163

Cooper, D. B., 66–68

Crown, Joe, 28, 29, 30, 31, 32, 37

Daniels, Art, 125

DEA. *See* Drug Enforcement Agency (DEA)

desegregation, 36, 51, 52, 53, 55

Dodson, Danny, 87, 92

Drug Enforcement Agency (DEA), 118, 127, 136, 137, 141, 148, 150, 151, 153, 154, 155, 161, 166, 169, 173, 180, 182

Duley, Ellis, 31, 33, 35, 83

Earp, Wyatt, 5, 29

Edmond, Rayful, 101, 115

Enforcement Operations Division caseload, 162

FIST operation, 168–169
jurisdictional disputes with FBI,
    164
major cases, 165–168
name change, 162
reputation, 161
stings, 158, 160, 168–170
Superbowl sting, 157–160
work with Interpol, 149

FBI
Background Investigation Con-
    tract Services, 174
comparison with Marshals Ser-
    vice, 164
D. B. Cooper investigation and,
    66–68
early dependence on Marshals
    Service, 34, 164
fugitive jurisdiction, 158, 161
Hostage Rescue Team, 73
involvement at Wounded Knee,
    90, 93
rivalry with Marshals Service, 164
Ten Most Wanted list, 118, 163,
    164
Federal Air Marshal Program, 60, 70
Fifteen Most Wanted list, 163, 167
FIST, 158, 168–169
Fountain Valley Five, 69, 129
fugitive apprehension
for Interpol, 146, 148–149, 152
Marshals Service's reputation for,
    162
national expansion, 161
transfer of responsibility from
    FBI, 158

warrants executed annually, 164–
    165
work with state and local agen-
    cies, 168
Fratianno, Aladena "Jimmy the
    Weasel," 137
Freeh, Louis, 182
Fromme, Lynette "Squeaky," 44

Goodfellas, 113
Grimm, Lloyd, 93
Gunsmoke, 5, 189

Hall, William, 3, 125
Hearst, Patty, 118
Hinckley, John, 1–4, 119
honorary marshals, 55, 171, 188–189

International Association of Chiefs
    of Police (ICAP), 145
Interpol
agencies involved, 147–148
annual conferences, 149–152
history of, 146
international fugitive hunting,
    148–149
Manuel Noriega and, 148
Marshals Service's role in, 148
name of, 145
National Central Bureau, 145
Investigative Operations. See En-
    forcement Operations Division

James, Chappie, 62–63
Johnson, Lyndon, 122

Kash, Reis, 107, 120, 125

Kennedy, Robert
    appointment of first chief mar-
        shal, 34–35
    comments on Ole Miss riot,
        51–52
    Marshals Service protection of,
        121–122
Kennedy, Ted, 121
Korea Gate scandal, 120
Kuffer, Chuck, 149, 160

LaBeet, Ishmael, 69
Leschorn, Bob, 158, 163, 167, 170
Lucas, Frank, 114

Marshall, Donnie, 182, 189
Marshall, John, 175–178, 180–181
Marshall, Thurgood, 175
Marshals Service. *See also* sky mar-
    shal program; Special Opera-
    tions Group; Witness Protection
    Program
    connection with federal courts, 2, 31
    creation of executive office, 35
    deputies killed in line of duty, 47
    desegregation efforts, 51, 53, 55
    Fifteen Most Wanted list, 163, 167
    history of, 5, 29, 31, 33
    Interpol activities, 148
    poor image of, 33
    prisoner transport, 41–47, 132
    role in civil disturbances, 74
    role in Washington, D.C., 36
Masterson, Bat, 5, 28
Matta-Ballesteros, Juan Ramon, 167
McKinney, Judy, 76, 122–123, 130,
    142

McKinney, Louie
    career with Marshals Service
        appointments as U.S. marshal,
            140–143
        as acting director, 182–190
        as chief deputy in U.S. Virgin
            Islands, 130–140
        as chief of Enforcement Op-
            erations Division, 103–113
        on D.C. warrant squad, 30–39
        as deputy director, 100, 102,
            179–180
        as deputy in Washington,
            D.C., 18, 21
        as Interpol representative,
            96–102
        prisoner transportation, 41–47
        as sky marshal, 57–66
        as SOG team member, 73–103
        as Witness Protection Pro-
            gram chief, 125–128
        as Witness Protection Pro-
            gram specialist, 105–125
    childhood
        effect of segregation on, 11
        early reaction to integrated
            life, 17, 49
        experiences in Asbury Park,
            New Jersey, 16–18
        farm life, 7–16
    early dissatisfaction with Mar-
        shals Service, 25–26, 28
    initial exposure to Marshals Ser-
        vice, 28–30
    naval enlistment, 18–23, 54
    as police officer in Washington,
        D.C., 26–28

McShane, Jim, 33–36
McVeigh, Timothy, 84, 188
Mengele, Josef, 168
Meredith, James, 29, 36, 51–52
Metropolitan Police Department,
    26, 28, 159
Moore, Luke, 29–30
Moore, Roger, 151
Morris, Stan, 160
Mulholland, Marty, 174

National Organization of Black
    Law Enforcement Executives
    (NOBLE), 145
Noriega, Manuel, 150

Oklahoma City bombing, 101, 152,
    187, 188
Operation Sunrise, 141
O'Toole, Jim, 125

Park, Tongsun, 120–121
Partington, John, 126
Persico, Alphonse "Allie Boy," 164,
    167
prisoner transport, 41–47, 132

racial profiling, 64, 189
Ramone, Mike, 176, 178, 179
Reno, Janet, 175, 176, 177
Rice Gate scandal, 120

Safir, Howard, 127, 146, 158, 165
Same, Graham, 51
Scotland Yard, 135, 151
Secret Service, 34, 119, 121, 148,
    151, 152, 153

September 11 attacks, 47, 58, 70,
    101, 103, 164, 187, 188
Shadow Stalkers, 74
Sheriff, Norman, 46–47
Shur, Gerald, 107, 108
sky marshal program, 59, 60, 62, 63,
    65, 66, 68, 188
Souter, David, 177
Special Operations Group (SOG)
    benefits to Marshals Service, 103
    deployments
        Alcatraz Island, 97–98
        Culebra, 99–100
        Danbury Prison, 99
        naval air station, 85–88
        overseas missions, 101
        Tocks Island, 98–99
        Vieques, 100
        West Virginia miner's strike,
            100–101
        Wounded Knee, 88–97
    general support of Marshals Ser-
        vice mission, 73, 101
    initial personnel training, 75–85
    nickname, 74
    origin of, 74
    post-hurricane efforts, 84, 133
    qualifications for personnel,
        74–75, 83
    security-related activities, 101,
        102
    support of FIST operations, 159
Stevens, John Paul, 177
Superbowl sting, 157–160

Ten Most Wanted list, 118, 163, 164
Thompson, Larry, 70

To Tell the Truth, 105, 127
Toomey, John, 147
Turple, Frank, 152

University of Mississippi, 29, 51–52
Urquidez, Rene Verdugo, 166
U.S. Navy, 18–23

Valachi, Joe, 106
Vandergrift, Frank, 31, 33, 36, 83
Virgin Islands, 68, 69, 84, 129–132,
   135–136, 142, 146–147, 149

Walsh, John, x, 170
warrant squad
   effect on Marshals Service, 32
   formation of, in Washington,
     D.C., 30
   nationalization of, 32, 161
   role of, 34
   warrants, 36, 38

Watergate scandal, 96, 119–120
Wilson, Edwin, 167
Witness Protection Program
   admission process, 109, 110
   early program names, 107–108
   family issues, 116
   initial problems, 108, 124
   leadership of, 125, 127
   organizational improvements in,
     125
   origin of Marshals Service's
     involvement in, 107
   protective services, 121–122
   role in high-profile cases,
     118–119
   skills needed by deputies in, 116
   successes, 106, 112, 113
   witness relocation, 111
Wounded Knee, 88–97

Young, Andrew, 128

About the Authors

Louie McKinney has enjoyed a long and distinguished career in law enforcement. In addition to being the first career deputy to lead the U.S. Marshals Service, he directed the service's fugitive apprehension unit (then known as the Enforcement Operations Division), received two presidential appointments as U.S. marshal for the U.S. Virgin Islands, and was the first African American to serve as chief inspector with Interpol. Louie is currently a director of MVM, Inc., a leading provider of uniformed protective services. He lives in Anne Arundel County, Maryland, with his family.

Pat Russo has more than twenty-five years of professional writing experience, including working as a writer and editor on the communications staffs of Fortune 500 corporations. He lives in northern New Jersey.